D0492953

Flowers from Seed

A CONCISE GUIDE IN COLOUR

Flowers from Seed

by *Jaroslav Průcha*
Illustrated by
František Severa

HAMLYN

LONDON · NEW YORK · SYDNEY · TORONTO

Translated by O. Kuthanová

Designed and produced by Artia for
THE HAMLYN PUBLISHING GROUP LIMITED
London · New York · Sydney · Toronto
Astronaut House, Feltham, Middlesex, England

© Copyright Artia 1976

All Rights Reserved. No part of this publication may be reproduced or
transmitted in any form or by any means, electronic or mechanical,
including photocopy, recording, or any information storage and
retrieval system, without permission in writing from the copyright
owner.

ISBN 0 600 33580 1
Printed in Czechoslovakia

3/02/25/51-01

CONTENTS

FOREWORD

It is impossible to imagine a life without flowers. Man's growing living standard brings an ever increasing need for flowers. True flower lovers, however, are not satisfied with buying blooms at the florist's but wish to grow them themselves. With some plants this is not easy, for their cultivation requires much care and labour. But there are many others that require practically no care at all. First and foremost of these are the annuals and biennials, which can be easily grown at little cost in every garden.

Looking at the emerging or fully grown blooms of many shapes and colours, watching the plants grow (some, such as ornamental gourds, or the twining plants of the morning glory, ipomoea, seem to grow under one's very eye) has a calming effect, particularly appreciated in the harassed and hurried life of our modern day and age. Working or sitting in the garden, even for a short while on coming home from work or during the weekend, is pleasant and relaxing.

This book gives a brief description of some of the most important species and the colour plates showing the most attractive examples of each are intended to facilitate making a choice from the vast assortment available on the market. The book is also designed to aid the reader in growing these plants successfully and to limit to the minimum possible failures, caused by the beginner's lack of knowledge of the basic requirements of the species.

ABOUT ANNUALS IN GENERAL

For practical purposes, flowers are divided into several groups and sub-groups such as annuals, biennials, perennials, greenhouse plants, bulbous plants and tuberous plants. These divisions do not correspond to the botanical classifications, and are often subject to change. Begonias *(Begonia semperflorens)*, for instance, formerly listed as greenhouse or carpeting plants are now generally classed as annuals.

Annuals are plants which complete their life cycle from seed to seed, that is they germinate, produce blossoms, then seeds and then die, within one growing season. In some plants this cycle covers a period of two years, even though the actual time between sowing and seed production is no more than twelve months. Such plants are called biennials. They are usually propagated by means of seeds, from which both species and varieties breed true. Also listed as annuals in catalogues are some plants that in their native habitats are classed as perennials. For example the snapdragon (antirrhinum) is a perennial in southern Europe and even in central Europe and elsewhere will sometimes last a number of years in a sheltered spot in the garden. The African daisy (dimorphotheca) is a perennial in South Africa and in Chile the same is true of the Marvel of Peru, *Mirabilis jalapa,* which forms black tuberous roots that can be overwintered in a shed sheltered from frost, like the roots of the dahlia. With all these plants propagation from seed is the easiest and best method.

Plants that flower mainly in summer but are propagated by vegetative means (pelargoniums, fuchsias) and are perennial when grown in the greenhouse are not considered to be annuals. Annuals and biennials are available in a large and diverse range of genera, are easy to obtain and require little care. Every year they provide a gay and colourful display outside the house or weekend cottage as well as on housing estates, in the grounds of factories and business companies, in parks and around school buildings.

Many of these plants produce long firm stems and a profusion of blossoms over a long period. When cut, they often last well in a vase. There are species and varieties of simple, delicate forms and others whose appearance, colour and perfume is more exotic. Many are less often seen at the florist's and as cut flowers simply because of their delicate structure and the difficulty of transporting them. Cultivation in the garden eliminates this drawback. When we grow our own flowers we can have a far greater selection of blooms and more chances to make imaginative arrangements of cut flowers for everyday decoration of the home as well as for festive occasions at far less cost than if we were to buy them.

FLOWER NAMES
AND THEIR SIGNIFICANCE

Some scientific names are of very ancient origin because the flowers were already known to the Greeks and Romans and were referred to in their myths and legends. Other names are more recent. Some flowers, for example, were named after the botanists who first described them or the collectors who discovered them in Africa, America or Asia and brought the seeds to Europe. Sometimes these flowers soon became established in their new environment, proved popular with gardeners and were widely cultivated. They were given new common names – either jumbled versions of the original names or ones that referred to some special characteristics of the plants. Because these common names show marked diversity, a uniform nomenclature, based on the plants' botanical classification and having the same meaning for experts of all nationalities, is essential.

Each designation consists of a generic name, such as *Amaranthus*, *Centaurea* and *Verbena*, and a specific name, for example *caudatus*, *tricolor*, *suaveolens*, *canadensis*, relating to the plant's origin or some other distinguishing feature (possessing a tail, three-coloured, fragrant, Canadian). Appended to the name is the intial of the botanist who first described the plant. In most cases the initial is L for Linné, the Swedish botanist who published a description of the said plants in his *Species Plantarum* in 1752. Another frequent abbreviation appended to the name is hort. for the Latin word *hortorum*, meaning grown and named in gardens.

International nomenclature is governed by systematics – a science which is continually developing and correcting its errors and inadequacies, thereby causing changes even in the scientific names of flowers. For example *Alyssum maritimum* now bears the name *Lobularia maritima, Chrysanthemum inodorum* is *Matricaria maritima* and *Matricaria eximia* is correctly classified as *Chrysanthemum parthenium*. The former names are given in parentheses as synonyms.

The issue of the International Code of Nomenclature, which recommends a system of rules and principles for naming plants, has resulted in the changing of the names of certain families that were not dervied from the generic name, for example *Gramineae* has been changed to *Poaceae, Cruciferae* to *Brassicaceae, Leguminosae* to *Viciaceae, Umbelliferae* to *Daucaceae, Labiatae* to *Lamiaceae, Compositae* to *Asteraceae*, and so on. These international rules are voluntarily observed by all botanists and authors of scientific works as well as books for the general public.

It might be of interest to see what the scientific designations mean and how some plants came to be given the common names they are known by.

The name *Ageratum* is derived from the Greek word *ageratos*, meaning unaging, forever young, and referring to the longlasting nature of the flowers. The newly opening blossoms cover the older faded blooms which are thus always hidden from sight. This characteristic is what gives the plant its name in Russian whereas the German name makes reference to the scent of the leaves. It has been grown in gardens since the 17th century.

The amaranthus bears flowers the whole summer long and faded blooms are never in evidence (the Greek word *amarantos* means unfading). The French and German names for *Amaranthus caudatus* compare the shape of the flowers to a fox's tail, whereas in English the shape and colour of the flowers have given it the name love lies bleeding.

The fact that the plant thrives in sandy soil is reflected in the name *Ammobium*, derived from two greek words – *ammos*, meaning sand, and *bios*, meaning life. The German and Russian names refer to the dry, almost papery aspect of the flower.

Antirrhinum is derived from two Greek words – *anti*, meaning resembling, and *rhinos*, meaning nose. In England the common name is snapdragon, but in other countries it is compared to a lion's, dragon's and hare's mouth. It has been grown in gardens since the 17th century.

Arctotis takes its name from the felty leaves (the Greek words *arktos*, meaning bear, and *otos*, meaning ear).

The name *Bellis* is derived from the Latin word *bellus*, meaning lovely, beautiful. In German the beauty of the flowers is multiplied a thousandfold, in

Czech only seven times. In Russian this flower is known as a small daisy.

Brachycome takes its name from the short hairs on the seeds (the Greek words *brachys*, meaning short, and *kome*, meaning hair). The English see in the flower a great resemblance to that of the daisy and their name for it is Swan River daisy.

Calendula, which in southern Europe flowers throughout the year, takes its name from the Latin word *calendae*, meaning first day of the month. The Germans call it ringelblume after the ring-like seeds, whereas in Austria it is known as totenblume, because the flowers are put in the coffins of the deceased and are used to make wreaths for All Souls' Day.

Callistephus chinensis, a plant whose seeds were brought to Europe from China in 1731, was first named *Aster chinensis* in reference to the single flowers reminiscent of the star-like flowers of the genus *Aster*. Since that time it has been known in many languages as the China aster. Not until 1833 was its name changed to *Callistephus*, from two Greek words – *kallistos*, meaning most beautiful, and *stephos*, meaning wreath, a name that does far greater justice to the extraordinary beauty of this flower. In France and Spain it is called queen of asters.

Campanula, or bellflower, takes its name from the characteristic shape of the flower (the Latin word *campanula* means bell). It is also known by this or a similar name in other countries. It has been cultivated in gardens since the 17th century.

The name *Celosia* derives from the glowing red colour of the blooms of certain species (the Greek word *celos* means fiery). It is interesting to note that *Celosia argentea cristata* is named in all languages after the shape of the flower which resembles the comb of a cock, hence cockscomb.

The name *Centaurea* comes from Greek mythology – the kentaur Chiron used the leaves of this plant to heal wounds. The English name, cornflower (and German, too) indicate that it is a weed of the cornfield.

The climbing stem of many species of *Convolvulus* is what gave the plant its name (the Latin word *convolvere* means to entwine). *Convolvulus tricolor*, grown as an annual, flowers only in the morning, hence its name in French – belle-de-jour. The German and English names, on the other hand, refer to the three-coloured blooms.

The name *Coreopsis* (from the Greek words *koris*, meaning tick, and *opsis*, meaning resembling – hence tickseed in English) does not evoke a pleasant image. The seed is to be blamed for this, for it is thought to resemble this unwelcome insect. Much better suited was the now no longer valid botanical title *Calliopsis*, meaning beautiful.

The name *Cynoglossum* is derived from two Greek words – *kynos*, meaning dog, and *glossa*, meaning tongue, in reference to the form of the leaves.

Delphinium comes from dolphin because of the similarity between the shape of the spur of its flower and a dolphin's body. Germans see in the spur a resemblance to a knight's spur, hence rittersporn, whereas the French compare it to that of a lark (pied d'alouette), as do the English (larkspur).

Pinks and carnations *(Dianthus)* have been grown in gardens the world over since the 15th to 16th century. According to Greek myths this flower is a gift of the gods, hence its name (*dios* meaning heavenly, divine, and *anthos*, meaning flower). The strong perfume of some species is reminiscent of the oriental *Caryophyllus aromatica.*

The name *Dimorphotheca* comes from two Greek words – *dimorphos*, meaning two-shaped, and *theca*, meaning fruit, because the plant produces two forms of seed vessels – rod-like and scale-like. The Russian, German and English names take note of the plant's African origin and resemblance to the flowers of marigolds or daisies.

Gaillardia takes its name from Gaillard de Marentonneau, a French nobleman and patron of botany. The German name refers to the colour of the flowers.

Gazania likewise takes its name from a scientist – Theodore Gaza – who lived in Rome in the 15th century. The German name takes note of the golden-yellow colour of the open blooms at noon.

The name *Gypsophila* (the Greek word *gypsos* means lime and *phila* means friend) tells us that this is a lime- or chalk-loving plant, frequently found growing on limestone cliffs. The German and English names refer to the plant's light and airy form.

Helianthus is known as the sunflower in all languages, being a literal translation of the Greek words *helios,* meaning sun, and *anthos,* meaning flower. The large flower heads resemble pictures of the sun.

The name *Helichrysum* comes from two Greek words – *helios,* meaning sun, and *chrysos,* meaning gold, which the colour of the flowers obviously calls to mind. The Russian and English names take note of their everlasting quality and the German and another English name (strawflower) refer to the dry bracts of the flower.

Chrysanthemum is composed from two Greek words – *chrysos,* meaning gold, and *anthemon,* meaning flower, and was so named because of the rich golden colour of many species.

Iberis is a native of Iberia, the old name for Spain, hence the botanical title.

Impatiens has seed pods that, when ripe, burst immediately when touched, hence the botanical title (the Latin word *impatiens* means impatient, sensitive).

Ipomoea takes its name from the twining character of the stem (the Greek word *ips* means worm and *homoios* means like). The English common name – morning glory – refers to the fact that it opens its blooms in the morning.

Kochia was named after the German botanist W. D. J. Koch. In Czech, Russian, German and English it is known as the summer cypress, referring to the characteristics of the plant.

The seed of *Lathyrus* was used by the ancient Greeks as a stimulant and hence the name (*la* means much, *thauros* stimulating). Other languages take note of the plant's scent and similarity to the pea.

Matthiola was named in honour of the famous 16th-century physician and botanist Pierandrea Mattioli, thanks to whom its cultivation spread widely.

Myosotis was so named because of the shape of the leaves (the Greek word *myos* means mouse and *otos* means ear). Common names in various languages have to do with the colour of the flower, namely blue, which is the symbol of faithfulness (in English – forget-me-not).

Mimulus has variously coloured flowers, hence the name taken from the Latin word *mimus,* meaning mimic. The common English name, monkey flower, sees in it a resemblance to a mask or monkey's face.

Mirabilis is unusual in that a single plant bears flowers of varied colours (the Latin word *mirabilis* means wonderful). The blooms, however, do not open until late afternoon and thus both the Russians and French call it beauty of the night.

Nicotiana was named after Jean Nicot, a French ambassador, who in the 16th century is said to have presented tobacco to the Court of Portugal. It is commonly known as the tobacco plant.

Nigella, grown in gardens since the 16th century as a spicey or medicinal plant, takes its name from the colour of the seeds (the Latin word *niger* meaning black). In some languages the common name compares the dainty foliage to a green veil.

The name *Petunia* was taken from the original Brazilian name.

The commonest species of the genus *Phacelia* has the flowers arranged in a cluster and the name is from the Greek word *phakelos*, meaning cluster or bundle.

The name *Phlox* is derived from the Greek expression for flame because of the brilliant glowing colours of its flowers.

Reseda was formerly used as a medicinal plant to relieve pain and hence its name (the Latin word *resedare* means to calm).

Translated, the Latin word *ricinus* means tick, the plant being so named because the seed is said to resemble this unpleasant insect.

Salvia was cultivated as a medicinal plant right back in ancient times. The name is from the Latin word *salvare*, meaning to heal.

Scabiosa is from the Latin word *scabis* meaning rough, a reference to the rough surface of the leaves of some species.

Schizanthus is from two Greek words – *schizein*, meaning cleft, and *anthos*, meaning flower, in reference to the shape of the petals. The English see in it a resemblance to a butterfly – hence butterfly flower.

Tagetes has been grown in gardens since the 16th century and takes its name from the Etruscan god Tages. Though it is a native of Mexico, the French call its tall forms rose of India and dwarf forms Indian carnation. The English and Czech consider Africa as the country of its origin, hence African marigold, whereas the German name alludes to the velvety surface of the petals.

Tithonia is derived from Tithonus, who in Greek mythology was loved by the Goddess Aurora.

Translated, the Greek word *tropaeolum* means small trophy because the flowers resemble a helmet (a battle trophy in ancient times).

Verbena is derived from the Latin word *verbum*, meaning word. According to Pliny the verbena was a sacrificial plant on which oaths were taken. It was considered sacred also in Persia.

The Latin *Viola* may be found already in the verses of old Roman poets as the name for violet. Both the Czech and German common names are derived from the word step-mother.

Xeranthemum is another flower that can be dried for winter decoration and the name is taken from two Greek words – *xeros*, meaning dry, and *anthemon*, meaning flower.

Zinnia was named after J. G. Zinn, professor of botany, and the flower is so called in many different languages.

CULTIVATION

Annuals, as a rule, are very easy to cultivate, having no special requirements. For each garden it is possible to select from the large number of species and varieties plants which will do well and produce a fine display of flowers. The development of the plant depends on the location, soil and climate. For any degree of success in growing flowers one must have at least a basic knowledge of these aspects and about the minimum requirements of the various species. Some, even though not particularly fussy, really will not thrive in certain conditions and the grower will have little success if he does not take their needs into account.

Tall, delicate plants put out in an exposed position are usually damaged by winds. Small, fine seeds will not germinate, as a rule, if sown in heavy soil that forms a crust; the young seedlings will suffocate. Plants requiring full sun are weak and spindly if put out in a shady spot and usually bear few flowers. Less hardy species are often frost-bitten and die soon after planting if put out too early in spring in areas frequently affected by late frosts.

However, even in such places it is possible to grow annuals with success if the right kinds are chosen. In windy sites we can plant low-growing species or provide a sheltering screen of open-work bricks or a dense planting of evergreens. In shady spots we can put flowers that are tolerant of shade such as *Impatiens holstii* or tuberous begonias. In locations where late frosts are not uncommon it is best to plant seedlings that have been hardened off in pots, waiting until the beginning of June to do so.

Situation

Most annuals and biennials do best in a warm, sunny site, only some species stand up well to partial shade. Of those described in this book only touch-me-not *(Impatiens holstii)* does well in a permanently shaded spot. Plants put in shaded sites are soft, spindly, flower poorly and are more susceptible to disease. Some species or varieties need to be planted in places sheltered from the wind, mainly those that branch close to the ground and form a fairly large bushy plant during the flowering period, for example zinnias, scabious and some forms of antirrhinum. The need for a warm, sheltered site depends on the location. Tender species may be grown with success even in colder areas if they are planted in a sunny spot beside a building, wall or fence that shelters them from cold air currents. Sometimes it is also possible to create a suitable microclimate for tender, dwarf species by planting them in front of a row of a fast-growing, larger species of annual such as summer cypress (kochia), castor oil plant (ricinus), malope or amaranthus.

Soil Cultivation

Most annuals and biennials have no special requirements as regards soil and will do well in any garden soil. Some species grow in truly poor soils and are very successful when used in the recultivation of soil on housing estates or in new gardens with less fertile soil that has not been cultivated for some years. Usually the application of adequate fertiliser is all that is needed. Only heavy, waterlogged soils are not suitable for growing annuals. Best of all are sandy, loamy, humus-type soils with good drainage and an adequate supply of nutrients. Most annuals also do very well in stony soil, which is often warm and well drained. For example, the China aster (callistephus) and annual statice (limonium), which do not like soil that forms a crust after rainfall, do very well in stony soil. Soil that forms a crust is less suitable for annuals and quite unsuitable for species grown from seed sown in the open. The character of such soil, however, can be gradually improved by the addition of peat, sand and well-rotted manure. Soil can be thus treated and made suitable for many species in a small area of a large, poor plot, this being frequently the case when laying out a new garden.

The direct application of fresh farmyard manure is generally not beneficial for most species. Their growth is too lush, they bear fewer flowers and are more prone to various diseases. Only stocks (matthiola) appreciate a light application of well-rotted manure in the autumn. Annuals should not even be provided with compost but should be put out in ground where a previously manured or composted plant has grown. Artificial fertilisers are applied according to need, best for this purpose being a general fertiliser applied at the rate of 1 1/2 to 2 ounces to a square yard. If the same or like species are grown in a single spot for several years, the soil becomes contaminated with various disease-producing substances, thereby making it impossible to grow some species in the garden for a number of years. For example, contamination of the soil with fusarium wilt often makes it totally impossible to grow China asters. In this situation, flower beds should be dug, preferably in the autumn, and the soil should be left unraked.

Sowing Seed Outdoors

Annuals are divided into species which can be sown outdoors where they are to flower and those that have to be hardened off first. Species sown in the open are first and foremost those that cannot be transplanted at all or do not transplant easily because they have a tap root, for example poppies (papaver) and the Californian poppy (eschscholtzia). Larkspur *(Delphinium consolida)* likewise does not transplant readily.

A great number of species can be grown successfully from seed sown in the open, though the plants are more vigorous and flower more profusely if grown under glass and hardened off before transplanting, for example the China aster (callistephus), common sunflower (helianthus), candytuft (iberis), clarkia, godetia and *Chrysanthemum carinatum*.

The method of sowing and time of sowing are determined by the requirements of the individual species as regards warmth of the soil, by the resistance of the young seedlings to frost, and by the desired period of flowering. Some species should be sown as early in spring as possible, as soon as the condition of the soil permits, so that the plants can become well rooted and attain a certain measure of growth before the hot, dry weather of early summer sets in. The seeds of other species are sown later when the soil is sufficiently warm or so that they will not germinate until the second half of May, when there is no longer any danger of late spring frosts.

April is the month for sowing seeds in the ground. The seeds of some fast-growing species can be sown in succession at one-month intervals from early spring until the beginning of summer, thus prolonging their flowering period. These include the marigold (calendula), cornflower (centaurea), clarkia, Californian poppy (eschscholtzia), godetia, toadflax (linaria), sweet pea (lathyrus), love-in-a-mist (nigella), poppy (papaver) and phacelia.

Some annuals can be sown in the autumn, but never

just before the soil freezes, for then the seed would not germinate. Seeds sown too early may germinate in warm, damp weather and such seedlings are then destroyed by winter frosts. If sown at the right time the seed will remain dormant during winter and germinate in spring (quite soon if the weather is favourable) and the resulting plants are more vigorous and flower more profusely. This method may be used for marigolds (calendula), candytuft (iberis) and Californian poppy (eschscholtzia). Autumn sowing is most successful in the case of delphinium.

Beds where annuals are to be planted must be well prepared in advance. Before sowing annuals the soil should be shallowly worked with a hoe or rake and artificial fertiliser should be added. Work should not be started until the soil is sufficiently dry, for otherwise it becomes too tightly packed and forms a surface crust, which makes further work difficult. Furthermore, plant growth is poorer in such beds. Seeds should be sown as soon as the ground is made ready so as to get the maximum benefit from soil moisture, particularly on lighter soil which has a tendency to dry out. If sown in dry soil germination is very unequal; for this reason it is best not to prepare all the beds in the garden at one time but only the required space just before sowing.

Seeds may be sown in rows, in small pinches or scattered over the area in question (broadcast). The third method is generally used only for sowing in seedbeds or when desiring to cover a large area with fast-growing species in place of turf. The best method is to sow in small pinches and in the case of very fine seeds in rows. Sowing in pinches or rows greatly facilitates further work such as thinning and weeding, especially in plots where weeds are rampant. Weeds usually germinate and grow much faster than the annuals and the newly emerging seedlings are much easier to distinguish from the young weeds when they are grown in specific rows or clumps.

The distance between rows varies according to the individual species but is usually 8 to 16 in. and is determined by the plant's habit of growth. The plants should be spaced so as to cover the ground as soon as possible but at the same time they should have sufficient room to develop. If planted too thinly the effect is not attractive, the soil becomes excessively dry or forms a crust and in windy weather the plants are more easily damaged. If sown too thickly the plants are weak, poorly developed and bear far fewer flowers. In some cases, however, such as clarkia, godetia and delphinium, it does not matter if the plants are spaced fairly close together for though they make few sideshoots the main stem bears a large number of flowers so that the effect in the flower bed is the same. This method is no setback even when growing flowers for cutting. Instead of cutting only the blooms, whole plants are cut or pulled up by the roots and then put in the vase.

Depth of sowing is determined by the size of the seed. A general rule is that the seed should be sown at a depth one and a half times greater than its diameter. The primary cause of failure in growing annuals is that the seeds are sown too deep, germination is unequal, sometimes with intervals of several weeks, and often they do not germinate at all. When sowing small seeds by hand the depth of the drill drawn with a peg or dibber is generally sufficient; seeds sown thus should not be covered with soil but simply pressed in. In the case of larger seeds the drills or hollows for pinches should be deepened with a hoe. The seeds are then covered with soil using a rake or hoe and the soil pressed down firmly.

The quantity of seed sown is determined by its powers of germination, time of sowing and character of the soil. In heavier soil it is better to sow in pinches because when a greater number of seeds germinate in a single spot the emerging seedlings push their way to the surface more easily than does a single plant. If seeds are sown too thickly the young seedlings are weak and their growth is poor even later on. For this reason sand or sifted ash is often added to very small seeds. Seeds should be sown in calm, windless weather for very light seeds such as those of the African daisy (dimorphotheca) may be blown out of the rows or hollows before one has time to press them in. Some seeds are a favourite food of birds. To prevent birds from eating the newly sown seeds care must be taken that none is spilt and that none remains in the neighbourhood of the bed.

Whether the soil in the bed should be pressed down

after sowing depends on the condition and character of the soil. Lighter soil should be pressed down firmly, heavier and moist soil should not be pressed down too much for this might result in the formation of a too-thick crust which would have an adverse influence on the growth of the seedlings. Provided that the weather in spring is not too dry, it is better not to water the beds. Once watering is commenced it is necessary to continue doing so until the seeds germinate for otherwise a crust might easily form on the soil surface and the emerging seedlings would suffocate. In the case of larger seeds the ground may be watered before sowing and the seeds then covered with soil.

Sowing in the Greenhouse and in a Frame

Even though a great number of annuals may be sown in their growing positions, many more must be sown in the greenhouse or under glass and gradually hardened off. Such plants are known as half-hardy annuals, and before deciding to grow these plants yourself from seed it is necessary to take into account whether you will have enough time and patience for the task. When we say that annuals are undemanding plants we refer to their requirements as regards location and care after planting out. No costly equipment is needed to grow good healthy seedlings and the work involved is fairly simple, consisting of providing the plants with water, air, shade and sometimes protection against frost. All these tasks must be performed at the proper time, depending on the weather and the requirements of the young seedlings. Too much ventilation in cold weather in the case of tender species or insufficient ventilation and high temperatures in the case of species requiring a cooler environment will cause poor results. In hot, sunny weather failure to lift the glass on just one occasion, or in the case of a severe frost, failure to cover it with straw matting, may mean that one's efforts are laid waste in a single day or night. However, with care and patience it is possible to grow a goodly number of seedlings by oneself – the reward being sturdy, beautiful flowering plants, either simple or exotic, and the joy and satisfaction of having raised and nurtured them from seed.

Young seedlings, however, may also be purchased at garden centres and from nurserymen. Generally available are begonias *(Begonia semperflorens)*, petunias, floss flowers (ageratum), snapdragons (antirrhinum), China asters (callistephus), sage (salvia), lobelia, African marigolds (tagetes) and zinnias, and of the biennials the English daisies (bellis) and pansies *(Viola tricolor)*. If one needs only a small number of seedlings and is content with the choice offered by the nurseryman, then buying them is by far the simplest and easiest method.

If you decide to grow your own seedlings you can take advantage of the large selection offered by seedsmen's catalogues or purchase the seed at a garden centre or chain store. Nowadays many gardeners have a small greenhouse or frame. They are comparatively easy and inexpensive to build if one uses transparent plastic sheet for the purpose. For earlier sowing it is necessary to dig a seedbed 16 to 20 in. deep, enclose it on all sides with boards (according to the dimensions of the glass top), cover the bottom with manure or autumn-raked leaves and top this with a 6 to 8 in. layer of finely sifted soil. For later sowing all that is necessary is to rake the bed to a fine tilth, enclose it with boards and cover with glass or plastic sheeting. Nowadays one can purchase ready-made plastic frames or greenhouses, incorporating a light, portable framework, in which seedlings can be grown with success, the only difference being that they probably do not afford as good protection against frost as does the fairly thick horticultural glass used for this purpose. This can be easily compensated for by covering the frame with straw matting or simply old, discarded sacks. The few species that need to be sown as early as January or February can be sown indoors in flower pots or seed trays placed on the window-sill and later transferred to a frame. Late annuals or biennials may be sown outdoors in a well-prepared bed in a warm and sheltered spot.

The time of sowing varies and is determined by the requirements of the individual plants. January to February is the time for sowing subjects that are slow to germinate or those that take a long time to grow before they flower, such as begonia, lobelia, phlox, salvia and verbena. March is the usual time for sowing seeds in a frame. Plants that grow fairly rapidly but are sensitive to frost should not be sown until April; these include amaranthus, cosmos, *Chrysanthemum carinatum*, mirabilis, tagetes and zinnia. Plantings from early sowings may easily grow too tall, especially in warm, sunny weather. These seedlings will be very slow to take root when planted out; also the grown plants will be weaker and less attractive. Most species root best in the early stage of growth and thus it is best to choose the time of sowing so that the seedlings are well developed but not too old when planted out. A few species can be transplanted during the flowering period; details are given in the descriptions accompanying the colour plates.

Boxes, pans and pots used for seed sowing must be clean, and should be thoroughly washed before use. John Innes seed compost or one of the peat-based composts are well suited for the purpose of seed sowing. The sowing medium in the boxes or flower pots should come to within about 1/2 in. of the rim and should be made moderately firm, leaving no gaps at the edges that would cause the young seedlings to dry up and die. The surface should not be pressed down but merely levelled with a piece of wood. Very tiny seeds need not be covered at all but merely pressed in with a small wooden board. Larger seeds should be covered lightly, best of all with a sprinkling of clean river sand. Under such a covering the soil remains sufficiently moist but the top dries quickly after watering and does not form a crust. The seeds germinate more easily and the seedlings are less prone to disease.

Sowing and hardening off in a frame is usually sufficient for most annuals. The bed where they are to be sown should be raked so that the surface is level and not, as so often happens, sloping at the same slant as that of the glass cover. In the latter case very fine seeds are often swept by watering to the bottom edge of the bed which is generally waterlogged, whereas the upper edge becomes unduly dry and the seeds germinate poorly, if at all. The seeds should be sown broadcast (scattered over the surface) or in rows. The ground should be watered using a watering-can with a fine rose so that it is kept uniformly moist and also shaded in sunny weather until germination has occurred. Shading is particularly important in the case of later sowings or in the case of biennials which are sown in May or June. The young developing seedlings are very tender and a single delayed watering means the end for them. Once germination has started less shade but more air is required and as for the amount and frequency of watering, that is determined by the weather.

Species with small seeds are generally sown too thickly and it is necessary to thin or prick out the young seedlings as they grow. In some cases, such as begonia, lobelia, and petunia, the seedlings are extremely small and are therefore pricked out in clumps the first time and individually at the second pricking out. For many annuals, pricking out is quite unnecessary; all they need is to be sown thinly, best of all in rows, and once they have germinated places where there are too many seedlings should be thinned. The soil between the rows should be hoed and kept free of weeds. This method is very good for cosmos, mirabilis, tagetes and zinnia.

Many annuals greatly benefit from pricking out. Such plants are sturdier, have a better root system, root more easily when planted out and also produce better growth. When pricked out, the roots should extend straight downward into the hole. Seedlings pricked out with roots bent have very slow, poor growth, this being especially true of stocks (matthiola), which should be pricked out with great care. Recently the practice of growing seedlings in peat pots is particularly effective for those plants which dislike disturbance. The plant roots soon fill the pots, making a nice rootball that need not be removed from the pot but is planted out in it. Plants that have been grown in such pots are not halted in their growth when planted out, take root quickly, branch well and bear flowers sooner. Planting into such pots is the same as when pricking out. They should be filled with soil, the young seedlings inserted so that the seed leaf is just above the surface and the soil then firmly pressed to the roots with a dibber.

Only species with similar requirements as regards heat and care should be put in the same frame. Snapdragons (antirrhinum) and stocks (matthiola), which require cool conditions, cannot be planted in the same frame as lobelia or verbena, which are sown and pricked out at about the same time but require comparatively more heat.

After they have been pricked out the seedlings should be given a·good watering so that the soil comes in contact with the roots, and in hot weather should be provided with shade for a few days and the soil kept adequately moist. As soon as the seedlings begin to grow they are no longer shaded but should be provided with more air and watered more thoroughly and less frequently. After the seedlings have attained a goodly size they are gradually hardened off by removing the glass and giving them more air both during the day and at night when the weather is warm so as to acclimatise them to open-air conditions – that is direct sunlight and alternating day- and night-time temperatures before planting out. Only seedlings that have been hardened off by leaving them without a glass cover for several days and nights should be planted out. If there is any danger or the seedlings becoming too tall it is a good idea to pinch out the growing point in time. Some species benefit by pinching out the growing point shortly after pricking out; they branch more rapidly and flower far more profusely, for example the floss flower (ageratum) and sage (salvia).

Only healthy and hardy seedlings with a good root system should be used for planting out. In the case of seedlings that have not been pricked out, care must be taken to cause as little injury as possible to the roots when removing them from the frame. The seedlings should be watered thoroughly the evening before they are planted out.

Planting out

The best time for putting seedlings out in the open is in the late afternoon in dull weather. Seedlings in peat pots or the like can be planted with success even under less favourable conditions, that is in dry and hot weather. The soil in which the seedlings are to be put must be prepared just as careflly as for sowing. Good and careful preparation of the soil pays off for the seedlings root well and quickly and this influences the plant's future development. At this time fertilisers should also be added to the soil. When the beds are ready the spacing is marked out with a marker or a garden line. For small areas or when planting smaller groups of various different species the distance, or at least the size of the grouping, can be easily marked with a dibber or rake handle. The spacing varies and is determined by the habit of growth of the given plants and the purpose the gardener has in mind.

Plants that are intended to stand out as solitary subjects, for example summer cypress (kochia) and castor oil plant (ricinus), or ones that are to be transferred to the beds from flower pots just prior to flowering, such as dwarf asters, are spaced farther apart so that the individual plants have room for growth. For borders, brightly coloured flower beds or spots that the gardener wishes to have covered as soon as possible after planting, the seedlings should be planted more thickly. If particularly large blooms are desired, for example with China asters or zinnias, the seedlings should be planted thickly, about 4 to 6 in. apart, and all the growing points pinched out leaving only one shoot. Spacing is also determined by the local soil conditions and climate. Plants have a much poorer, weaker growth in less nourishing soil at higher, cooler elevations than in good nourishing soil at lower elevations in a warm, sheltered site. The best spacing for each illustrated species under normal conditions is given in the descriptions accompanying the colour plates.

Seedlings in peat pots are planted with the aid of a garden trowel. Seedlings that have been pricked out as well as those that have not are planted with the aid of a dibber. When doing so care must be taken to injure the roots as little as possible, to place them so they are not bent, and to press the soil firmly round the roots. A good way of testing if the seedling is planted properly is to try to pull it up by a leaf; the leaf may tear but the seedling should remain firmly in the ground. After being planted out the seedlings should be given a liberal application of water. Once they have begun to grow, they should be checked frequently and watered when necessary.

It is important to know the correct time for planting out the various species in their flowering positions. Many annuals are natives of tropical regions and do not tolerate frost and therefore can only be put out in the open after all danger of frost is past, that is at the end of May and in some areas not until the beginning of June. In the case of species sensitive to frost it is better not to be in too great a hurry – often just one single light frost may mean total loss of the plants overnight. This important aspect is also included in the description of the individual species. Peat pots are particularly suitable for these sensitive subjects, for they can be planted out later, when there is no longer any danger of frost, without the growth or period of flowering being influenced in any way. Some species, such as stocks (matthiola) and *Phlox drummondii*, on the other hand, thrive in the damper weather of April (light frosts leave them unharmed), whereas if planted out in warmer weather at the end of May they develop into weak plants bearing few flowers.

Biennials should be planted out in time to take good root before the onset of winter. Weak, poorly rooted plants, sometimes also ones that have grown too much, are not as good at overwintering. The weather is often unsuitable when biennials are being planted out and this must therefore be done with that much extra care. Until they begin to show signs of growth, the plants must be watered liberally. Some species grown as biennials are frequently planted out into a temporary bed in the autumn and transferred to their flowering positions the following spring. In this case they are spaced fairly close together because a smaller area is more easily managed.

Care and Cultivation of Plants

Seedlings grown directly from seed must be thinned in time. Sections that are too crowded are best thinned twice, leaving a greater number of seedlings in place during the first thinning and thinning a second time when it is certain that the remaining seedlings are developing nicely. The second thinning should leave two seedlings at the most in one spot and when the process has been completed the soil should be pushed up close to the remaining plants. By this time the weather is often quite hot and if left exposed the white necks of the small seedlings might be scorched, leaving the bed bare and black the following day.

In rainy and dull weather the thinned-out seedlings of some species may be replanted to fill in gaps.

Further care of annuals is fairly simple. They should be watered as necessary, preferably with sufficient water being applied to soak right down to the roots and not just a light sprinkling. The best time of day to water is in the early morning or towards evening. Some species are extremely tender when watered on a hot sunny day, for example *Delphinium consolida*, love-in-a-mist (nigella), Californian poppy (esch-scholtzia) and marigold (calendula), and often die as a result.

Furthermore, weeds should be removed regularly and fertilisers added as required. Soil that forms a crust after rainfall or after watering should be kept open by hoeing, according to need, so that the plants can breathe. Some species, such as the China aster (callistephus), are particularly sensitive in this respect.

In some species the flowering season may be prolonged by prompt removal of faded flowers to prevent seed formation. In the case of sweet peas (lathyrus), for instance, the flowering period may be prolonged until autumn. Some species, if trimmed by about one-third after flowering, will produce a second crop of flowers, provided they are watered and supplied with fertilisers. Examples are coreopsis, lobularia and nemesia. Some plants are particularly attractive to wild rabbits and hares and cannot be planted where these animals have access. Pinks put in such a site must be fenced in immediately after planting. Other annuals rabbits like to nibble are *Helipterum roseum*, gazania, xeranthemum, tagetes, lobelia, kochia and some species of verbena.

Supports for twining and climbing plants should be made ready before sowing or before putting the seedlings in their flowering positions. In most cases it is not necessary to fasten the plants to the supports. As soon as the seedlings start to grow all that needs to be done is to press them against the support with soil or tie them to it only at one point and they will continue climbing by themselves.

Biennials should be protected against frost with a light covering, preferably of fir branches, which, however, must be removed early in spring so that the plants do not die.

Pests and diseases which attack ornamental plants are described and dealt with in detail in various publications. The commonest pests of annuals and biennials are aphids, particularly in the case of the China aster (callistephus) and the poppy (papaver). The best means of protection is to spray the plants with a suitable chemical, following the manufacturer's instructions carefully.

INTRODUCING NEW SPECIES AND VARIETIES

The number of individual species and varieties is continually increasing. Every year, new varieties are being introduced and others again vanish from the scene, only to reappear some time later, either in the same or only slightly modified form. Like clothes and jewellery, flowers, too, are influenced by fashion, though at lengthier intervals. Some species that were cultivated in many separately coloured varieties some forty to fifty years ago are nowadays grown only occasionally and then only in a mixture of colours, for example hollyhock (althaea), *Delphinium consolida,* opium poppy *(Papaver somniferum), Phlox drummondii* and trumpet flower (salpiglossis). Other species, unknown years ago or cultivated only occasionally, are now available in many varieties, such as touch-me-not *(Impatiens holstii)* and African marigold *(Tagetes erecta).* Examples of annuals that were once widely cultivated, then lost their popularity and in recent years have been 'rediscovered' are ornamental gourds (cucurbita), ornamental grasses and some species of sage, *Salvia coccinea, S. farinacea* and *S. horminum.*

At first the selection of cultivated annuals was enlarged mainly by gathering and importing them from various parts of the world. Many species are grown as ornamentals in the same form as they grow in their native habitat. Others, however, are so altered that they show no resemblance whatsoever to the original forms. Many new and frequently very attractive varieties have resulted from chance interbreeding. Also marked differences between the plant's original and new environment have sometimes resulted in the development of new varieties. Even so, the assortment of species remained comparatively limited. However, Mendel's discovery of the 'law of heredity' a hundred years ago marked an important turning point. Since then the patience and skill of plant breeders has given us a great many new strains with new colours and larger and differently shaped flowers. Nevertheless, many of the breeders' aims still remain unrealised. Two examples are the efforts to develop China asters that would be resistant to fusarium wilt and to grow a white African daisy, both of which have met with very little success to date. The breeding of new hues, as yet absent in the colour range of various species, has in many instances been unsuccessful or else the results have not corresponded to what the breeder had in mind. New ways and means are being sought and tried in the endeavour to solve these and many other problems. Seeds, flowers and whole plants are soaked, sprayed or watered with various chemical agents. In recent years even X-ray and radiation have been used and the effects followed up.

Far greater success has been achieved with (and far greater use made of) the discovery that first generation hybrids exhibit complete uniformity and generally flower more profusely and for a much longer period. Frequently they also have larger blossoms than the parents and are more resistant to bad weather and various diseases. In seedsmen's catalogues such forms are often called F_1 hybrids. Another distinguishing characteristic of these forms, besides the above excellent traits, is that the seed produced from this progeny will not reproduce the characteristics of the parents – further generations will lack either the colour, the size or the fullness of the blooms. Plant breeders and seedsmen take advantage of this fact to protect their interests and safeguard their secrets.

Employed with great success in the breeding of *Matthiola incana annua* has been the combination of double-flowering qualities and chlorophyll-producing qualities which has yielded hundred per cent. double strains giving ample seed production as well. Several days after germination it will be found that the seed leaves of the matthiola seedlings show differences in colour, some being a lighter green than the others. (If this difference is not sufficiently pronounced the temperature in the frame should be lowered to 10 °C and the boxes with the seedlings exposed to light for 10 hours.) When pricking them out, only the light green ones should be transplanted, for these are the doubles, the ones with dark green leaves being single-flowered plants.

GROWING PLANTS FOR SEED

Some species or varieties can be grown with success from seed harvested in one's own garden. Sometimes this can be done several times in succession. However, to avoid the disappointment and failure that may lie in store for the gardener growing plants from his own seed it is generally best to buy fresh seed every year from a reliable firm. This applies in particular to varieties of unusual shape, colour or size of bloom, which differ markedly from the original form and cannot be grown repeatedly from their own seed. To obtain good-quality seed it is not enough to select and mark out a nice, attractive plant, harvest the seed and sow it. The development of the seed and its qualities are influenced by a great many different aspects; some of these effects may be observed in the poor habit of growth or poor quality of flowers the same year the seeds are harvested whereas others – which is far more unpleasant – not until the following year.

Plants grown for seed have much greater climatic requirements than other plants. The best areas for growing annuals for seed are warm, sunny regions with a low annual rainfall. The site should be sheltered from strong winds for the seeds of some species do not ripen at all in areas with rough, cold weather, and abundant rainfall during the flowering season stands in the way of successful pollination and results in the production of very few seeds.

Plants produce seed after pollen has been deposited on the stigma. In some plants the pollen is transferred from the anther of a flower to the stigma of the same flower (self-pollination), whereas in other instances the plant must be pollinated with pollen from another flower (cross-pollination). Some species of the latter type will not become pollinated with their own pollen, which makes it necessary to pollinate them by artificial means in the case of a solitary specimen from which we wish to harvest seed.

To prevent undesirable pollination it is necessary to isolate the plants. The simplest method, though difficult in the garden, is to isolate the plant by spacing. For wind-pollinated plants the distance should be greater – 350 to 600 yards, for insect-pollinated plants a spacing of 55 to 220 yd. suffices. In the case of some species it is necessary to keep in mind the possibility of pollination by pollen from related weeds. Such plants include amaranthus, *Viola tricolor* and bellis. Where fewer seeds are required a single plant (sometimes even a single flower) may be isolated with cheese-cloth, thick wire mesh or simply a paper bag pricked full of holes. In the case of self-pollinated species, all that needs to be done is to mark the selected plants and harvest the seed separately. Of course, the possibility of self- or cross-pollination varies according to the individual varieties, and is determined by the form of the flower; for example, the double forms of China aster (callistephus) are generally self-pollinated whereas single or semi-double forms may sometimes cross-pollinate one another quite easily.

The seeds of annuals usually ripen in succession, depending on the order in which the separate flowers bloom, and thus should also be harvested in the same sequence. Frequently the seeds are apt to fall out after they are ripe and should therefore be harvested as soon as they have ripened. Prematurely harvested seeds have very poor powers of germination. In some instances it is wise to wait until the seeds begin to fall from the first flowers to be certain they are ripe enough. As soon as the seeds begin to ripen the plants should be checked more frequently in order to harvest the seeds properly and in time. In some species the seed does not fall out so easily when ripe, whereas in others it does so very quickly. The seeds of some plants, such as sweet alyssum (lobularia) and lobelia, are harvested even though the plant is still covered, to a great extent, with blooms. Those of other plants must be harvested as soon as possible to prevent birds from devouring the whole crop, for example cosmos and centaurea.

The harvested seeds should be spread out to dry on a sheet of paper in a dry and well-ventilated room. The seed pods of pansies and balsams (impatiens) are green when harvested and should therefore be spread out in a thin layer so they don't become mouldy. Because the seeds of these plants are scattered a fair distance when the ripe pods burst it is furthermore necessary to cover them with wire mesh or lightweight, loosely woven fabric. Polythene bags are not suitable for storing seeds that are not sufficiently dry for they easily become overheated in the moist microclimate that forms inside the bags or else become mouldy and do not germinate. Harvested plants, fruits, or ovaries generally release the seeds quite easily when fully dry and larger bits of the dry plants or flowers may be easily separated from the seeds by sifting the latter through a mesh. Round seeds can be cleaned by rolling them back and forth on a piece of glass or hard paper. When growing seeds for sowing in one's own garden it is not necessary to be particularly thorough about cleaning them, a task that is often very labourious. It is enough to make a guess as to how many good seeds the cleaned amount contains and sow accordingly. Seeds sold on the market must measure up not only to certain standards as regards powers of germination but also as regards cleanliness, and the latter are often very strict indeed.

The packets into which the cleaned seeds are put should always be marked with the name of the plant and year of harvesting so that the gardener can tell at a glance how long they may be stored if he doesn't plan to sow them the following year. The table on pages 68–70 gives the number of seeds per gram as well as the approximate period during which the seed can be successfully sown (will still germinate) for the individual species. The power of germination and its durability are greatly influenced by the conditions under which the seed ripened. Seeds that ripened in fine, dry weather generally germinate much better and retain this power longer than seeds that ripened in rainy weather. The seeds of some species germinate very poorly immediately after being harvested and will do well only some one to three months later.

USES OF ANNUALS
AND BIENNIALS

Certain of the better-known species of annuals have been used for years past for the decoration of parks (tagetes, *Salvia splendens*) as well as cemeteries (pansies, forget-me-nots and begonias), but the place where the wide range of these plants can really come into its own is in the garden.

People often think an annual is a plant with a fairly short flowering period. Though some species do flower only very briefly a suitable selection of species and varieties and sowing the seeds at different times can provide a bright display of colour from early spring till late autumn. True, they must be planted out every year, sometimes even several times during the year, but the seeds and seedlings can be obtained at comparatively little cost and in most cases the plants are of very simple cultivation. If one knows the several basic requirements such as the place and time of sowing, type of location, size of the plant and period of flowering (all this information is generally printed on the seed packet), then even the beginner can be successful in growing certain species. Annuals flower 8 to 10 weeks after sowing so that possible mistakes caused by the unsuitable location of a plant or use of an unsuitable species may be corrected the very same season. When planting perennials such a thing is much more difficult, for in this case a mistake may not become evident until some years later.

When selecting the species and varieties to be grown in the garden it is necessary to keep in mind the conditions of the given site and the purpose the ornamental beds are intended to serve. If they are located in front of the house or below windows they will be fairly wide, whereas those situated alongside paths or turf will be narrow. Tall plants are very good as screens or hedges to separate the kitchen garden or mask walls and fences. They grow rapidly and within a comparatively short time form an attractive backdrop with their fresh green foliage as well as blooms. Besides, these flowering hedges will often provide ample cut flowers for the house throughout the summer. Very good for this purpose are althaea, amaranthus, cleome, cosmos, helianthus, kochia, malope, nicotiana, ricinus and tithonia.

Popular plants for the quick covering and shading of tall archways, pergolas, walls and fences are ipomoea and *Phaseolus coccineus*, which grow rapidly and bear flowers until late autumn. Lathyrus may also be used to good advantage for this purpose but the flowers should be removed as soon as they fade before they start to make seed. The best support for climbing plants is a coarse wire network but just as good is a taut string or wire, or the pickets or poles of a fence.

Annuals do not receive the full appreciation they deserve as plants for the rock garden or ornamental wall. Even though many people will object that annuals do not belong to a proper rockery yet one often sees rock gardens that are a mass of colour in spring and sometimes also in the autumn but have a very meagre display of flowers in the summer months. This is where many annuals come into their own, ones that differ little in size from the other plants in the rock garden but whose bright blooms provide a colourful feast for the eyes in summer. Naturally, one must leave room for such plants and their placing must be done with care so that they harmonise with the overall scheme. Sometimes there need be no more than one or two plants or a small group, depending on the size of the available space and the dimensions of the rock garden. Annuals are very good fill-ins for patches left bare after the spring bulbs have finished flowering. Recommended for the rockery are dimorphotheca, dorotheanthus, gazania, *Limonium suworowii*, linaria, lobularia, mimulus, nemesia, phacelia, *Phlox drummondii*, portulaca, sanvitalia and silene. Plants that do very well between stone or cement paving blocks in dry locations as well as in dry walls are dorotheanthus, linaria, lobularia, portulaca, sanvitalia and silene. Low, dry slopes alongside access roads can also be brightened and made more attractive by planting low-growing species that tolerate dry conditions and full sun. Recommended are convolvulus, dimorphotheca, dorotheanthus, lobularia, phacelia, *Phlox drummondii*, portulaca, sanvitalia and verbena.

Some annuals can be used to brighten dull corners,

for example in a bed of newly planted perennials while the latter are becoming established. Lobularia, for instance, sown amidst roses or gladioli, will brighten the green expanse of their foliage before they bloom.

Annuals are invaluable for window-boxes, in tubs on a balcony, in earthenware urns on terraces and on pedestals, on stair landings as well as for public areas. Though generally of wood, window-boxes may be made of all kinds of different materials. Polystyrene and other plastics have been gaining in popularity in recent years. They are light, durable, provide good insulation and protect the soil and plant roots from direct sunlight.

Growing plants in containers is the same as in flower beds; the only thing that has to be kept in mind is that the containers dry out much more rapidly and the soil temperature is usually higher. The soil in the container must be nourishing and not too finely sieved so that it does not become too firmly packed when watered frequently. Best of all is a mixture of loam, sand and peat or one of the proprietary soilless composts. The containers must have drainage holes in the bottom which should be covered with sand or broken crocks and rubble so that they do not become clogged and surplus water can flow off. It is especially important to remember to make holes in the bottom when making occasional use of a metal or other container. Too little moisture is not good for plants but on the other hand if surplus water cannot escape the soil soon becomes waterlogged and turns sour, causing decay of the roots.

Containers should be filled with soil several days before planting so that the soil has time to settle. When the seedlings have been planted the soil should come to within 3/4 in. of the rim to allow for adequate watering. On slanting window-sills, wedges should be pushed under the boxes so that they are level and the soil is uniformly watered; besides this they should be securely fixed with a piece of wire so they will not be dislodged by wind. Water should be applied according to need, with a liquid fertiliser added at regular intervals according to the manufacturer's instructions. The surface should be loosened with a stick now and then and the plants sprayed lightly with water to wash the dust off.

Large containers in courtyards and the like may be filled with taller plants such as amaranthus, kochia and ricinus, but generally recommended for boxes are small, bushy plants that bear a great profusion of flowers and stand up well to the vagaries of the weather and lack of moisture. Ideal for this purpose, besides the usual petunias and begonias, are a number of very attractive flowering annuals such as iberis, impatiens, dorotheanthus, nemesia, mimulus, portulaca and verbena. Full-grown plants as well as ones that are in bud or full flower can also be put out into containers, for example ageratum, low-growing forms of callistephus, celosia, lobelia, lobularia, salvia, *Tagetes patula* and *tenuifolia, Viola wittrockiana* and low-growing forms of zinnia. Climbing and rambling plants such as ipomoea, lathyrus, *Phaseolus coccineus* and tropaeolum are also good for balconies and patios. In a larger space and an adequately sized container it is possible to plant even ornamental gourds (cucurbita) – forms that bear small fruits. Supports for climbing plants should be put up in good time, before the plants begin to grow.

The greatest possibilities, however, are afforded by borders, in other words flower beds of varied width and length alongside paths, buildings, below windows or in grass. These beds may be planted with one type of plant of the same colour, a mixture of several species of the same colour, one type of plant in various colours, or a mixed assortment of several species and varieties. With a bit of careful planning it is possible to choose species that will flower when one can enjoy them most. For example, in the weekend cottage garden, which is usually visited at length during the summer holidays, one can put out plants that flower most abundantly during the summer months. If one's time in the garden is limited to the afternoons then it is not a good idea to plant flowers that open in the morning and close in the afternoon (gazania, dorotheanthus), but rather those that give a good display throughout the day or open in the late afternoon (mirabilis, nicotiana).

It is possible to have a bed of small plants, medium-sized plants or tall plants or one with plants of varying height. The selection and arrangement depend on the site and on the distance of the bed from the viewing point. Narrow beds are usually planted with an eye to being viewed from above or from one side; wide beds are planted to produce a good effect from both sides either with subjects of the same height or with taller plants in the centre and shorter ones at the edges. Narrow borders alongside paths where the flowers can be viewed at close range may be planted

Fig. 1. – Mixed bed of low-growing annuals.

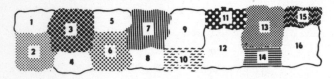

1. *Tagetes patula* – brown, single; 2. *Mimulus luteus* – mixture, yellow-red; 3. *Verbena rigida* – violet; 4. *Sanvitalia procumbens* – yellow; 5. *Verbena hybrida* – white; 6. *Verbena hybrida* – red with white eye; 7. *Lonas inodora* – yellow; 8. *Lobelia erinus* – blue; 9. *Salvia splendens* – scarlet; 10. *Tagetes patula* – yellow, double; 11. *Phlox drummondii* – cream; 12. *Gazania splendens* – mixture; 13. *Lobularia maritima* – violet; 14. *Tagetes patula* – orange, double; 15. *Verbena hybrida* – pink; 16. *Verbena hybrida* – blue with white eye.

with a mixture of different species. With careful thought it is possible to have one or more species always in bloom and to allow an opportunity of examining at close quarters flowers that are often very interesting but which appear nondescript when viewed from a distance (see Fig. 1).

If the bed is to be viewed from a distance it should be planted with fewer species and varieties, ones with larger and more brightly coloured blooms set out in masses. An attractive idea in beds alongside paths, in grass or beside a wall, is a ground cover of low-growing, spreading plants interspersed at regular intervals with clumps of eight to ten tall plants (Fig. 2). Smaller areas, such as a bed in a corner of the lawn beside a path, can be planted with different plants at different times of the year. Biennials, or plants treated as such, planted in the autumn and flowering in

Fig. 2. – Simple border beside a path – clumps of 8 to 10 taller plants with ground cover of low-growing bushy species.

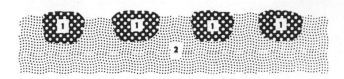

1. *Cosmos bipinnatus* – pink
   or
1. *Salvia farinacea* – blue
   or
1. *Salpiglossis sinuata* – mixture

2. *Phlox drummondii* – white

2. *Petunia hybrida* – pink

2. *Lobularia maritima* – white

early spring may be followed by plants put out at the beginning of June which flower in late summer (Fig. 3). A similar method is shown in Fig. 4, where the selection starts with species sown outdoors in early spring, which when they have finished flowering (some time in the middle of August) are replaced by biennials that flower the following spring.

With some knowledge of the characteristics of the various plants, their flowering periods and habits of growth, it is possible to grow a large number of species even in a small space and have a continuous display of colourful blooms throughout spring and summer. For instance, one can plant alternating rows of clarkia, crepis, *Limonium suworowii*, *Iberis umbellata*, *Matthiola annua*, nemesia, papaver, phacelia, schizanthus, all of which have rapid growth and flower very early, and species that develop more slowly and flower

Fig. 3. – Bed in a corner of the lawn beside a path.

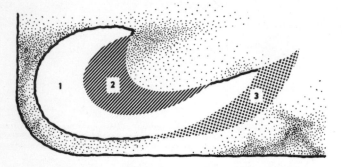

Autumn planting for spring flowering; 1. *Viola wittrockiana* – yellow: 2. *Myosotis alpestris* – blue, *Tulipa hybrida* – yellow; 3. *Bellis perennis* – pink. Spring planting: 1. *Sanvitalia procumbens* – yellow; 2. *Salvia farinacea* – blue; 3. *Lobularia maritima* – pink; or 1. *Salvia splendens* – scarlet; 2. *Rudbeckia hirta* – yellow; 3. *Ageratum houstonianum* – blue.

later, such as callistephus, *Dianthus chinensis*, gaillardia, mirabilis, rudbeckia, scabiosa, *Tagetes erecta* and *Verbena hybrida*. It is not necessary, however, to plant whole rows in this manner; it is also possible to plant or sow amongst the later-flowering plants a few earlier-flowering species. These should be plants with large, vividly coloured blooms that will brighten the comparative monotony of the others' green foliage. After the flowers have faded the plants should be removed with care, or else trimmed down hard, so that the later-flowering species can develop properly (Fig. 5).

In Fig. 6 is a fairly mixed bed consisting of species that need to be hardened off and are put out as late as

Fig. 4. – Bed with plants sown where they are to grow – short-flowering period.

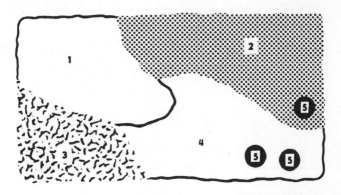

1. *Delphinium consolida* – pale violet; 2. *Clarkia elegans* – white; 3. *Godetia hybrida* – red; 4. *Crepis rubra* – pink; 5. *Kochia scoparia trichophylla* – single specimens. Mid-August planting of biennials for spring flowering: 1. *Campanula medium* – white; 2. *Dianthus barbatus* – red; 3. *Bellis perennis* – pink; 4. *Viola wittrockiana* – blue.

the end of May. When planting such beds care must be taken to ensure that the individual plants do not conceal one another and that the habit of growth and colour of the various species harmonise to form an attractive arrangement. Calendula, cosmos and ursinia, for example, are quite unsuitable companions for *Begonia semperflorens.* Very effective as eye-catchers or subjects for punctuating the landscape are certain tall species planted singly, in small patches in the lawn, in front of a building or against a backdrop of tall shrubs. Some are selected for their ornamental

Fig. 5. – Bed with plants sown where they are to grow – long-flowering period.

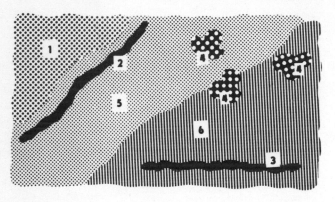

1. *Eschscholtzia californica* – yellow; 2. *Papaver somniferum* – pink (the row conforms to the outline of the patch; after the flowers have faded the plants can be pulled out); 3. *Iberis umbellata* – white (one row; when the flowers have faded the plants can be pulled out); 4. *Linum grandiflorum* or *Malope trifida* – red (clumps of 3 to 5 plants); 5. *Lobularia maritima* – white; 6. *Lobularia maritima* – violet (the lobularia will fill in the gaps left by the pulled-out plants).

foliage or habit of growth – kochia, ricinus – others for their ornamental foliage and brightly coloured, sometimes fragrant flowers – amaranthus, cleome, cosmos, helianthus, nicotiana, tithonia, *Salvia farinacea* and *Verbena bonariensis.*

Further examples of the many various ways in which

annuals can be used are shown in Fig. 7 and 8. The assssortment in Fig. 7 was selected with an eye to the site, the plants either flowering the whole summer long or else flowering one after the other. Fig. 8 shows a similar arrangement; in this case, however, it is a

Fig. 6. – Mixed bed of long-flowering plants.

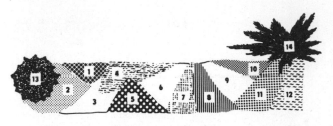

1. *Salvia coccinea* – red; 2. *Ageratum houstonianum* – blue; 3. *Gazania splendens* – mixture; 4. *Lonas inodora* – yellow; 5. *Salvia splendens* – scarlet; 6. *Verbena rigida* – violet; 7. *Lagurus ovatus* – silvery; 8. *Verbena hybrida* – violet with white eye; 9. *Verbena hybrida* – pink; 10. *Verbena bonariensis* – pale violet; 11. *Xanthisma texanum* – yellow; 12. *Verbena hybrida* – red; 13. *Tamarix pentandra*; 14. *Juniperus virginiana tripartita*.

country garden in front of windows, where the various species will flower in succession, account being taken of the fact that some will be cut for home decoration. Many annuals can be used for cutting. Fig. 9 shows a bed which will provide flowers for cutting the whole summer long. Most species will benefit if the first blooms are cut so that the later ones can develop well.

Growing annuals in one's own garden makes possible a wide choice of flowers for cutting. These include numerous lovely annuals which are very attractive for indoor decoration but which are not

Fig. 7. – Beds of annuals in the immediate vicinity of the house.

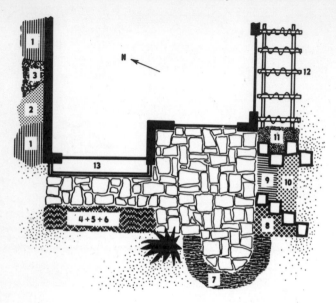

1. *Impatiens holstii* – pink; 2. *Impatiens holstii* – red; 3. *Lobelia erinus* – blue;
4. *Lagurus ovatus* – silvery; 5 *Nicotiana sanderae* – red, fragrant; 6. *Salvia
farinacea* – pale blue, fragrant (mixture of species 4, 5, 6 with preponderance
of lagurus); 7. *Tropaeolum majus* – scarlet; 8. *Sanvitalia procumbens* – yellow;
9. *Lobularia maritima* – white; 10. *Portulaca grandiflora* – mixture;
11. *Dorotheanthus bellidiformis* – mixture; 12. *Ipomoea purpurea* – red,
climbing; 13. *Petunia hybrida* – pale pink, in a box.

available in the shops because they have small or
tender flowers, short stems, and the like. Many of
these plants bear a great profusion of blooms so that
even the cutting of large quantities makes no
noticeable gap in the bed, for example calendula,
low-growing or small-flowered varieties of calliste-

Fig. 8. – Country garden in front of the house windows.

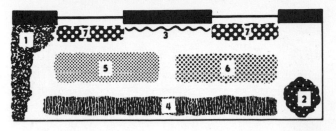

1. *Althaea rosea* – mixture; 2. *Helianthus annuus* – yellow (1 to 3 plants);
3. *Lathyrus odoratus* – pale blue, climbing; 4. *Tropaeolum majus* – yellow;
5. *Callistephus chinensis* – mixture; 6. *Antirrhinum majus* – mixture; 7. *Reseda odorata* – fragrant.

phus, centaurea, cosmos, gaillardia, chrysanthemum, lathyrus, nigella, scabiosa, *Viola wittrockiana* and small-flowered varieties of zinnia. Often only a few blooms, such as those of the large, ornamental quilled varieties of callistephus or some delicate, pastel-coloured sweet peas placed in a suitable vase, are all that is needed to create a pleasant and festive atmosphere for special occasions. Very striking for table decoration are the flowers of annuals which are usually only seen in the garden from a distance or else borne on a large plant amidst dense foliage. Single malope or tropaeolum blooms are very effective in small, shallow dishes whereas whole salpiglossis or schizanthus plants make a striking display in round vases, mainly thanks to the prominent veining and unusual shape of the flowers. Attractive bouquets of various harmonising hues can be made with large-flowered varieties of *Centaurea moschata* or

Fig. 9. – Bed of annuals good for cutting.

1. *Dianthus chinensis* – white; 2. *Rudbeckia hirta* – yellow; 3. *Scabiosa atropurpurea* – pale blue; 4. *Scabiosa atropurpurea* – dark purple; 5. *Antirrhinum majus* – pink; 6. *Antirrhinum majus* – white; 7. *Gaillardia pulchella* – red together with yellow; 8. *Gaillardia pulchella* – reddish brown; 9. *Callistephus chinensis* – quilled, pink; 10. *Callistephus chinensis* – quilled, pale blue; 11. *Zinnia elegans* – yellow; 12. *Lagurus ovatus* – silvery; 13. *Tithonia rotundifolia* – orange; 14. *Pyracantha coccinea* – orange fruits in the autumn.

several different shades of *Scabiosa atropurpurea.* Many annuals go very well with other species of ornamental plants in modern ikebana-style floral arrangements. Very suitable for this type of arrangement, which generally consists of only a few blossoms, twigs or plant parts, are the ornamental grasses agrostis, lagurus and panicum. *Nigella damascena* and *Verbena bonariensis* can be used for ikebana arrangements even after the flowers have faded.

The lifespan of cut flowers varies and depends mainly on the given species. Cutting at the proper time and the ensuing care can extend the life of blooms to a remarkable degree. The best time for cutting is early in the morning when it is still cool and the plants are saturated with water and freshened by the dew, or else in the evening. Flowers cut in the heat of the day when the plants have transpired moisture will not last as long. Some annuals may, or even should, be cut when the flowers are only partly developed or still in bud. Such flowers then open gradually in the vase. Flowers that are cut in full bloom and are already pollinated do not last long. *Papaver somniferum,* centaurea, dianthus, lathyrus and scabiosa should be cut while still in bud or only partially open; matthiola, too, should be cut when about a third of its flowers are in bloom. Other species, on the contrary, should be cut in their prime, for example most members of the family *Asteraceae* – cosmos, coreopsis, helianthus, rudbeckia, venidium and zinnia, as well as *Phlox drummondii.* The flowers of arctotis will not open at all in the vase if cut prematurely. Also, flowers cut while it is raining will not last long, especially ones with a delicate structure, for they are easily damaged. Leaves should be removed from stems that are to be put in water, for if submerged they decay very rapidly. Water in the vase should be changed daily. To increase the stem's power of absorption it is best to cut the end at an angle with a sharp knife when changing the water. The lifespan of cut flowers can be improved by the addition of certain chemicals which may be obtained from a florist.

Gaining in popularity in recent years are annuals that retain their shape and colour when cut and dried. They may be used, together with dried ornamental grasses and twigs of evergreens, for home decoration in winter when fresh flowers are scarce. Suitable flowers for drying include helichrysum, *Helipterum roseum*, *Limonium bonduellii*, *L. sinuatum*, *L. suworowii*, Ionas and xeranthemum. The flowers should be cut when the blooms are nearly full but before they are past their prime for otherwise when dry some of the small florets may fall or turn black. The cut flowers should be tied up in small bunches and left hanging upside down in a shaded, well-ventilated room until thoroughly dry. Dried flowers will preserve their colour better if they are immersed in a proprietary dessicant.

Besides being decorative in the garden some annuals, such as centaurea, clarkia, cynoglossum, *Iberis umbellata*, phacelia, reseda and salvia, are also a favourite food of bees.

Annuals can be used for the same purposes and in the same ways in parks and on housing estates as in the garden. Fewer varieties and colours but greater masses are used when putting plants out in larger areas. Mixed beds have been gaining in popularity in recent years even in public places, consisting of either only annuals or annuals together with bulbs, pelargoniums and other plants. The same general rules apply here as for growing annuals in the garden in the selection of plants, care and cultivation with regard to their special requirements and the combination of plants for various layouts. However, parks and housing estates do not afford as much leeway for experiments as does the small garden. Even though things can be put right fairly easily in the event of a failure by putting out new plants, the gardener's efforts are submitted to greater and more critical scrutiny by many more people than in one's own small garden.

In the decoration of such areas it is possible to take advantage of the fact that some annuals can be grown in pots or reserve beds until they begin to flower – for example low-growing species of China aster and pansies – and then transferred, either just before they reach maturity or in full bloom, to their final location. Some fast-growing species, such as convolvulus and tropaeolum, can be sown directly where they are to flower and will provide good ground cover for large areas until such time as other, more permanent arrangements are laid out or have time to grow.

There is no denying the fact that despite their brief life annuals and biennials have many advantages. They are easy to cultivate, produce flowers in a very short time and bear a great profusion of blooms in a wide range of bright colours, some of them being true gems. They are ideal plants for the beginner without any experience in gardening, giving him the opportunity to try his hand and see the results of his efforts quite quickly and at the same time to acquire knowledge and experience that he can put to good use in growing more difficult plants later on.

Most Important Characteristics of the Seeds of Annuals

	Number of seeds per gram	Powers of germination	Where to sow	Seed will germinate in
		years		days
Ageratum houstonianum	6,000–7,000	2–3	G GF	7–10
Agrostis nebulosa	10,000	2–3	GF	5–7
Althaea rosea	80–90	3	GF	10–14
Amaranthus caudatus	1,500	4	O GF	10
Ammobium alatum	1,500–1,900	2	GF	7
Antirrhinum majus	6,000–8,000	4	G GF	14
Arctotis grandis	450–550	3	GF O	14
Begonia semperflorens	75,000	2–3	G	14
Bellis perennis	7,500	2–3	GF	10–14
Brachycome iberidifolia	6,000	3	GF	7
Calendula officinalis	150–170	4	O	6–11
Callistephus chinensis	450–500	3	GF O	7–10
Campanula medium	4,500	3	GF	14
Celosia argentea	1,100–1,300	3–5	G GF	5–7
Centaurea cyanus	250	3–4	O	8–14
moschata	300–350	3–4	O	8–14
Chrysanthemum carinatum	300–350	2–3	O GF	8–14
coronarium	500–600	2–3	O GF	8–14
parthenium	6,500	2	GF	6–12
segetum	300–400	2–3	O	8–18
Clarkia elegans	3,000	2–3	GF O	5–10
Cleome spinosa	4,000	2–3	GF	14
Convolvulus tricolor	80–100	3–4	O	10–14
Coreopsis drummondii	700	3	GF	6–12
tinctoria	2,000–3,000	3	GF	6–12
Cosmos bipinnatus	150	2–4	GF O	6–14
sulphureus	120	2–4	GF O	6–14
Crepis rubra	700	2–4	O	10–14
Cucurbita pepo	14–18	2–4	GF O	7–10
Cynoglossum amabile	300	3	O	10–21
Delphinium consolida	400–600	4	O	14–21
Dianthus barbatus	1,000	4	GF	14
caryophyllus	600	4	GF	10–14
chinensis	1,000	4	GF	10
Didiscus coeruleus	350	2–3	GF	10–16
Dimorphotheca sinuata	550–650	3	O	6–10

	Number of seeds per gram	Powers of germination	Where to sow	Seed will germinate in
		years		days
Dorotheanthus bellidiformis	4,000	2–3	GF	7–14
Eschscholtzia californica	400–500	2	O	10–14
Gaillardia pulchella	400–500	2	GF	8–14
Gazania splendens	200–250	2	GF	7
Godetia grandiflora	2,000	4	GF O	7–12
Gypsophila elegans	1,000	2	O	7–14
Helianthus annuus	20–50	3	O GF	10–14
Helichrysum bracteatum	1,300–1,500	3	GF	7
Helipterum roseum	380	2–3	GF	7
Iberis amara	350	5	GF	6–8
umbellata	400	5	GF O	6–8
Impatiens balsamina	100	6	GF	6–8
holstii	2,000–3,000	6	GF G	6–8
Ipomoea purpurea	40–50	2–4	O GF	7
Kochia scoparia	1,000	2–4	O	7–14
Lagurus ovatus	4–6 sprays	2–4	O GF	14–18
Lathyrus odoratus	12–15	3–4	GF O	10–14
Limonium sinuatum	10–15 fruits	2–3	GF	10–14
suworowii	4,000–5,000	2–3	GF	10–14
Linaria bipartita	12,000–13,000	2	O	10
Linum grandiflorum	300	5	GF O	7–10
Lobelia erinus	33,000–50,000	2	G	10
Lobularia maritima	2,500–3,000	3	GF O	7
Lonas inodora	3,000	3–4	GF	10
Malope trifida	250–300	4	O	6–8
Matthiola incana	600	2–3	G	7
Mimulus luteus	23,000	2–3	GF	7–14
Mirabilis jalapa	10	2–3	GF	10
Myosotis sylvatica	2,000	3–4	GF	14
Nemesia strumosa	4,000–5,000	2	GF	6–12
Nicotiana alata	6,000–8,000	4	GF	7–14
Nigella damascena	450–500	2–3	O	10
Panicum capillare	2,000–3,000	2–3	GF O	7–14
Papaver rhoeas	7,000–8,000	3–4	O	7–10
somniferum	3,000	3–4	O	7–10
Pentstemon hybridus	2,000–2,400	2–3	GF G	14–21
Petunia hybrida	7,000–9,000	4	G	15
Phacelia campanularia	2,000	3	O	14
Phaseolus coccineus	800 per kg	4	O	14
Phlox drummondii	460–550	3	G GF	7–10

	Number of seeds per gram	Powers of germination	Where to sow	Seed will germinate in
		years		days
Portulaca grandiflora	9,000–10,000	4	G	5–9
Reseda odorata	1,000	3–4	O	12
Ricinus communis	3–6	3–4	GF O	7–14
Rudbeckia hirta	2,500	3	GF	5–9
Salpiglossis sinuata	4,500	4	O GF	7–10
Salvia coccinea	700–800	3	GF	9–14
farinacea	800–900	4	GF	9–14
horminum	300–400	2–3	GF	9–14
splendens	350	2–3	G	9–12
Sanvitalia procumbens	700–1,000	2–3	GF	10
Scabiosa atropurpurea	160	3	GF	6–10
Schizanthus wisetonensis	1,800–2,000	2–3	GF	7–10
Silene pendula	900–1,000	3	GF	7–10
Tagetes erecta	250	2–3	GF	8–12
patula	400	2–3	GF	8–12
tenuifolia	1,400	2–3	GF	8–12
Tithonia rotundifolia	90	2–4	GF	4–8
Tropaeolum majus	10–20	4	GF O	10–12
Ursinia anethoides	1,000	2–3	GF	6–10
Venidium fastuosum	1,300–1,500	2–3	GF	6–12
Verbena bonariensis	4,000	1–2	GF	10–14
canadensis	1,500	1–2	GF	10–14
erinoides	800	1–2	GF	10–14
hybrida	300–400	1–2	G	10–14
rigida	1,200–1,500	1–2	G	14–21
Viola wittrockiana	800–1,100	2	GF	7–14
Xanthisma texanum	760	2–3	GF	7–14
Xeranthemum annuum	700–800	2–3	GF	7
Zinnia angustifolia	500	4	GF	7
elegans	120–150	4	GF	7

ABBREVIATIONS:

G – in the greenhouse in a seedbox
GF – under a glass frame
O – outdoors in flowering position

PLATES

Ageratum houstonianum

Asteraceae
(Compositae)

Syn. *A. mexicanum* SIMS.

Floss Flower

4 to 24 in.

June to October

The original species *Ageratum houstonianum* is a native of Mexico, where it grows as a perennial semi-shrub up to 2 ft. high. The leàves are toothed, heart-shaped to ovate, vivid green, covered with a light down. The densely clustered cymes are made up of small and larger flower heads of white, pink or generally blue, tube-shaped florets. In full bloom they completely cover the leaves. Only a few varieties attain a height of 1 1/2 to 2 ft. and are used for cutting, for example 'Tall Blue', 'Blue Bouquet'. Most varieties, however, are very short, 4 to 8 in., for example 'Blue Cap' and 'Blue Mink'. All bear a profusion of flowers and even when grown from seed their growth is fairly equal. Greater uniformity of habit and more abundant flowers are qualities for which the new F_1 hybrids bred in recent years are particularly noted, such as 'Blue Blazer', 'Blue Heaven' and 'North Sea'.

Ageratum does best in well-drained soil in a warm, sunny situation. If watered sufficiently and provided with a dressing of fertiliser the plants will be a decorative feature in the garden the whole summer long.

The seeds should be sown in February in boxes under glass, where they will germinate within a week. The seedlings should be pricked out into boxes and later into peat pots or else thinly spaced in a glass frame. The growing points should be pinched out once or twice so that they make good lateral shoots. The hardened-off seedlings should be planted out in the second half of May (they are sensitive to frost), spaced 6 to 10 in. apart. The flowers appear shortly after and the flowering period lasts until late autumn.

Ageratum has many uses. Taller varieties are planted in borders and for cutting. Low-growing varieties are useful as an edging plant and are often used as bedding plants in parks. They are also grown in flower pots, boxes on balconies and earthenware urns for the decoration of public areas in cities.

Agrostis nebulosa BOISS and RENT

Cloud Grass

Poaceae
(Gramineae)

12 to 16 in.

July to August

Of the many species of this genus the one used for decoration is *Agrostis nebulosa*, which grows wild in western and southern Europe. The plants are up to 16 in. high, airy and very ornamental. The leaves are short and often tightly rolled. The tiny, single-flowered spikes are borne in delicate, richly branched panicles that are narrow at first and gradually expand as the seeds ripen.

Cloud grass does well in any good garden soil in a sunny situation; it also tolerates semi-shade. The seeds should be sown in April in boxes or in a frame and need not be covered with soil. The plants may be pricked out or planted outdoors in small clumps. Plants that have been hardened off may be put out in their flowering positions about 8 in. apart at the beginning of May. Plants may also be grown from seed sown in the open but this method is not recommended, for the seeds are very fine and germination is poor.

Cloud grass is planted in the crevices of rock walls, alone in patches or together with taller perennial grasses. The light and airy flowers are also useful for cutting and are attractive both fresh as well as dried.

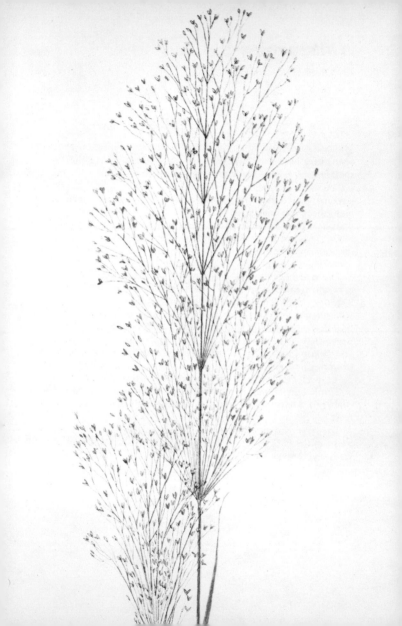

Althaea rosea CAV.

Hollyhock

Malvaceae

5 to 8 ft.

July to August

Althaea rosea, the most widespread and most important species, is probably a native of Syria. It is generally cultivated as a biennial but sometimes will grow for a number of years in one site.

The large, roundish, heart-shaped, palmately lobed leaves form a ground rosette from which rises the stem, sometimes as much as 8 ft. high, the upper half bearing a spike of large showy flowers – single, semi-double as well as double. All green parts of the plant are rough and felted. The flowers measure 3 to 4 in. across. The double varieties are the most widely cultivated and are listed in seedsmen's catalogues according to the colour of the blooms.

The hollyhock may be propagated by cuttings and division but is generally grown from seed. This should be sown under glass or in a seedbed at the end of May or beginning of June, where it germinates within ten days. The young seedlings should be pricked out and after they have been hardened off planted outdoors in early September where they are to flower (spaced 2 to 3 ft. apart), or else in a temporary bed (spaced 8 to 12 in. apart), whence they are transferred to their flowering positions in spring. The plants should be provided with a light cover, preferably of fir boughs, as protection against frosts.

The hollyhock requires nourishing, loamy soil and a warm, sunny, sheltered situation. In soil that is exceedingly wet it is easily killed by frost.

The large, showy plants are very effective when planted in groups in grass, at the back of simple beds in a cottage-type garden or to mask walls and fences.

Amaranthus caudatus L.

Love Lies Bleeding

Amaranthaceae

2 to 3 ft.

August to October

Of the many amaranthus species native to tropical Asia and Africa those that are good as ornamentals are *A. caudatus*, *A. paniculatus* and *A. tricolor*. *Amaranthus caudatus* is of robust habit and grows to a height of 2 to 3 ft. The leaves are elliptic to ovate with long stalks and are coloured dark red in the sun. *A. c. atropurpureus* has long, drooping racemes of small, purplish-red flowers. There is also a pale green form – *A. c. viridis*. Varieties of *A. tricolor* ('Joseph's Coat') grow to a height of 2 to 3 ft. and have decorative crimson, yellow and green leaves and insignificant flowers.

Amaranthus requires a light, nourishing, humus-rich soil with adequate lime content and a warm, sunny situation.

A. caudatus and *A. paniculatus* should be sown outdoors in their flowering positions in May or in a cold frame in April, the hardened-off seedlings then being planted out at the end of May in their flowering positions, 1 1/2 to 2 ft. apart. The plants do not tolerate frost. *A. tricolor* is more sensitive than the other species. It should be sown in boxes in a greenhouse in mid-March and the hardened-off seedlings planted out at the end of May spaced 1 1/2 ft. apart.

All the above species are used for planting in mixed beds, alone in separate beds, in front of fences as well as in earthenware urns.

Antirrhinum majus L.   *Scrophulariaceae*

Snapdragon

8 to 36 in.

June to September

Antirrhinum majus is native to southern Europe and Asia Minor, where it grows as a perennial but is not completely frost-resistant. Currently available varieties are treated as annuals, even though in mild winters they will grow in one site for a number of years. The stems are thickly covered with glossy, entire leaves. The individual flowers on short stems are arranged in dense or thinner spikes and bloom in succession.

Breeding has yielded a great number of varieties of many different colours and two of the more important are *A. majus maximum* and *A. m. grandiflorum;* both are good for cutting. The plants are 2 1/2 to 3 ft. high, of branching habit, with dense spikes of medium-sized flowers. Available also are scientifically raised F_1 hybrids that are good for forcing. Suitable as bedding plants and for planting in boxes and bowls are the intermediate varieties of antirrhinum. In most forms the main and lateral stems develop at the same rate and attain practically the same height – 16 to 24 in. The spikes of fairly large flowers are quite long and often quite dense. Varieties of the *A. majus pumilum* group are of branching habit, only 6 to 8 in. high, with short spikes of small flowers.

Snapdragons thrive in nourishing, sandy, loamy soil with good drainage and in a sunny site; tall forms should be provided with protection against winds.

The seed should be sown in boxes in the greenhouse in February or March. Hardened-off seedlings may be planted out as early as mid-April, spaced 10 to 14 in. apart.

Snapdragons are excellent for cutting. They may be planted in large or small groups in parks and gardens, also in boxes and flower bowls.

Arctotis grandis THUNB.

African Daisy

Asteraceae
(Compositae)

6 to 40 in.

June to October

Of the many species that are in the main native to South Africa, *Arctotis grandis* is the one of importance as an ornamental. It is a white-felted plant with vigorous habit of growth, branching abundantly from the base and attaining a height of 2 to 3 1/2 ft. There may be as many as fifty flowers on a single plant, opening in succession over a long period. They measure 2 to 3 in. across and are coloured white, with delicate violet shading on the reverse of the petals and a blue-violet central disc of tube-shaped florets. The stems are firm and quite long. Also available in addition to this species is *A. hybrida* hort. – a mixture of pastel-hued daisies 10 in. high.

Arctotis requires a light, well-drained soil and warm, sunny position. It is intolerant of wet soil and is only really good when it has lots of direct sunlight. The flowers open in the morning, shortly after dawn, and close in the afternoon. In rainy weather they remain closed the whole day. Late in the autumn, however, they are open continuously. Cold and rainy weather has a very adverse effect on the plant's development.

Seeds should be sown under glass at the end of March and hardened-off seedlings planted out 12 to 16 in. apart in the middle of April.

Its long flowering period and wealth of blooms makes arctotis very good for mixed beds, borders and cutting.

Begonia semperflorens

LINK and OTTO

Begoniaceae

6 to 14 in.

May to October

The various species of this genus are widespread in the tropical and subtropical parts of America, Africa and Asia. Most are popular for the greenhouse and home decoration. Cross-breeding has yielded the *Begonia semperflorens* hort. varieties which grow as perennials but are treated as annuals. Varieties of the *B. gracilis* group are low-growing plants of thickly branched habit with smaller flowers. Varieties of the *B. semperflorens* group are characterised by more vigorous growth and fewer flowers, but the blooms as well as the leaves are larger than those of *B. gracilis*. Seedsmen's catalogues furthermore list the separate varieties according to height (tall, intermediate and short) and also according to whether they have green or red foliage. The flowers are white, pink and red. Generally listed in seedsmen's catalogues, apart from only a few of the older varieties, are forms classified as F_1 hybrids which are characterised by uniformity of habit, wealth of flowers, continuous flowering and greater hardiness.

Begonias do best in a warm, sunny position in well-drained soil containing plenty of humus.

Seeds should be sown in late December or during the month of January in pots or trays. Growing the seedlings requires a great amount of care and it is therefore often better to buy the young plants from the nurseryman. They are generally planted out when already in bloom, spaced 6 to 10 in. apart, at the end of May, because they do not tolerate frost.

Begonia semperflorens is chiefly used in parks and gardens as an edging and border plant as well as in mixed beds, boxes and earthenware urns.

Bellis perennis L.

Meadow Daisy

*Asteraceae
(Compositae)*

4 to 10 in.

April to July

Bellis perennis, native to Europe, is a small plant with small, single blooms. From this plant have sprung various garden forms which are more robust and bear larger blooms. Though resembling a single flower the flower heads are made up of numerous florets which are of two types: tongue-shaped and tube-shaped. The many varieties have been divided into several groups, or strains, according to the size and type of flower; for example 'Pomponette' with miniature, double blooms; 'Double Monstrosa' with large, semi-double blooms; 'Monstrosa Super Giants' with flowers up to 3 in. across; 'Double Red Quilled Etna' with large quilled blooms. The flowers may be white, pink, red or a combination of two colours. In recent years breeders have produced F_1 hybrids of this plant, too.

Meadow daisies grow best in nourishing loam and in a sunny situation. In soil that is too wet they decay or freeze easily.

The seeds should be sown at the end of June or beginning of July in boxes or under glass and should be shaded until they germinate so that the soil does not become too dry. Hardened-off seedlings may be moved at the end of August or in September to their outdoor places, where they should be spaced some 12 in. apart. As a rule, however, they are put 6 to 8 in. apart in beds where they overwinter, and then transferred to their flowering positions the following spring. They should be provided with a light cover of evergreen twigs as protection against frost. The flowering period is from the end of April until the beginning of July.

Meadow daisies are very popular as bedding and border plants, for window and balcony boxes and for earthenware urns. Some varieties may be used for forcing for home decoration in vases.

Brachycome iberidifolia BENTH.

Swan River Daisy

Asteraceae
(Compositae)

8 to 10 in.

June to September

Brachycome iberidifolia is native to Australia. It is about 10 in. tall, thickly branched, with fine, dainty leaves. The pleasantly scented flowers measure about an inch across; the outer petals roll up as the flowers fade. The colour is blue-violet, red-violet or white, with a blue-black or yellow-brown central disc.

The Swan River daisy does best in well-drained, dryish soil with ample nutrients and in a warm, sunny position. It is intolerant of damp soil and mature plants are greatly damaged by lengthy periods of rainy weather.

The seeds should be sown at the end of March or during the month of April under glass or in boxes where they will germinate within a week. The seedlings should be pricked out in time and watered with care. After they have been hardened off the seedlings should be planted out in their flowering positions, 8 to 12 in. apart, in the second half of May. They begin to flower at the end of June and in sunny weather produce flowers throughout the summer.

The Swan River daisy is used for mixed beds, borders and in boxes on balconies.

Calendula officinalis L.

Pot or **Garden Marigold**

Asteraceae
(Compositae)

1 to 2 1/2 ft.
June to September

Calendula officinalis is a native of southern Europe, where it was grown for its medicinal properties as early as the 12th century. A sturdy plant of branching habit, it grows to a height of 20 to 30 in. The flower heads are 3 to 4 in. across and are borne on long, firm stems. Generally cultivated are the double varieties such as 'Chrysantha' – canary yellow; 'Baby Orange' – orange, semi-double; 'Pacific Beauty' – creamy white, golden yellow, dark orange; 'Golden King', 'Orange King' and 'Art Shades' – a mixture of colours, as well as semi-double forms with pronounced dark centres.

Calendula is an adaptable plant and does well in practically any soil with sufficient lime and in a sunny position.

The seeds should be sown in April outdoors where they are to flower and the plants thinned to 12 to 16 in. apart, but they may also be sown in a cold frame. The seedlings root very well and in the case of plants sown outdoors those that have been thinned out may be transplanted to other positions. For earlier flowering the seed may be sown in autumn. The flowering period may be extended by removing the blooms as soon as they have faded. If seed is allowed to ripen the blooms that appear later are semi-double or single and the plant ceases to bear flowers. Large double blooms may be obtained by cutting away all side growths.

The pot marigold is very popular for cutting and will last 5 to 8 days in water. However, the flowers should be cut before they are fully open. Calendula is often used for mixed beds in country gardens as well as in separate groups in parks. The glowing colours are very attractive even from a great distance.

Callistephus chinensis (L.) NEES

China Aster

Asteraceae
(Compositae)

8 to 36 in.

July to October

Callistephus chinensis is a native of China. The original species was about 2 ft. high with single white flowers. Over the years, however, breeding has produced many types that differ in height, number of branching stems, habit of growth, shape and size of the flower heads and shape and arrangement of the florets. The various colours also embrace a wide range – orange and black as well as all the other hues in many different shades. Some varieties are even bicolored.

The many varieties are generally placed in separate groups to aid selection, the main ones being according to the flowering season (early, semi-early and late-flowering varieties) and according to height (tall, intermediate and dwarf). These are furthermore divided according to the shape, size and arrangement of the florets in the flowerhead. In seedsmen's catalogues the list of available asters covers several pages but here we shall name only the better known ones, namely the 'Princess' strain, 'Pompon', 'Perfection' and 'Ostrich Plume'.

Asters grow best in nourishing, loamy, sandy soil and in a sunny position. They are intolerant of fresh farmyard manure and wet soil and should be planted in different sites each year to prevent the possibility of attack by fusarium wilt. (It is also recommended that varieties resistant to this disaease should be selected).

The seeds should be sown in March and April under glass and the seedlings planted in the open 10 to 16 in. apart at the beginning of May. Light spring frosts will not harm the plants. The seed may also be sown in April where the plants are to flower but then blooms are borne much later.

Asters have many uses. Cut flowers will last 8 to 10 days in water. Low-growing varieties may be transferred to flower pots and balcony boxes just before flowering.

Campanula medium L.

Canterbury Bell

Of the many species of bellflower, most of which are perennial, the only one of importance as a biennial is *Campanula medium* – the Canterbury bell, a native of southern Europe and France. The fairly large, petioled leaves with toothed margin make a good-sized ground rosette the year the seed is sown, followed in the spring of the next year by a branching stem up to 3 ft. high bearing pyramidal panicles of large, bell-like flowers from the end of June until August. The colours are white, pink, pale blue and dark violet. Varieties are available in separate colours and in a mixture of colours. They are divided according to the shape of the flower into three groups: single; double cup and saucer (no longer the characteristic bell shape); and hose in hose or calycanthema (with corolla and calyx the same colour).

Campanula does best in nourishing, loamy soil and in a sunny situation. It is intolerant of excessive damp and is readily damaged by frost.

The seeds should be sown thinly in a cold frame or seed bed in June. If sown more thickly the seedlings should be thinned in time and then they need not be pricked out. Hardened-off seedlings may be moved to their outdoor places in August or the beginning of September and should be spaced 16 to 20 in. apart. To overwinter well they must be well rooted and should also be provided with a light cover of evergreen twigs as protection against severe frosts. This should be removed as soon as growth starts the following spring.

Campanula is very striking and decorative. It is planted in mixed beds, as a single subject in grass, in groups in front of ornamental shrubs and also in beds of perennials. It is good for cutting, with the buds opening in succession.

Celosia argentea cristata   *Amaranthaceae*

O. KUNTZE

Syn. *Celosia cristata* L.   6 to 32 in.

Cockscomb   July to September

Of the many species of *Celosia* widespread in the warm regions of
Africa, America and Asia, the most important is *C. argentea,* from
which two horticultural forms have sprung. One is *C. argentea cristata,*
6 to 16 in. high, with flower heads 6 to 10 in. across, available in several
separate colours – yellow, pink, red, brick-red and violet. The other is
C. argentea plumosa (syn. *C. pyramidalis plumosa*), an erect plant of
branching habit with feathery flowerheads of narrow, pyramidal shape.
The plants grow to a height of 8 to 32 in. but most widely cultivated are
the low-growing to intermediate forms (8 to 10 in. tall).

Cockscomb grows best in warm, well-drained soil with a good supply
of moisture and nutrients, and in a warm, sunny position. In cold and
rainy weather it has very poor growth.

The seeds should be sown in the greenhouse in boxes or in a cool
frame in March or early April. Growing seedlings is fairly difficult and
does not always meet with success, sometimes making it necessary to
sow seeds anew. The seedlings are intolerant of frost and therefore
cannot be moved outdoors until the end of May, where they should be
spaced 8 to 12 in. apart.

Cockscomb is used for planting in pots, in boxes on balconies, in
earthenware urns and in separate groups in parks and public areas.
Inasmuch as seedlings hardened off in pots transplant very well, they are
often used as bedding plants to follow spring flowers that have faded.

Centaurea moschata L.

Syn. *Amberboa moschata* (L.) DC.

Sweet Sultan

Asteraceae
(Compositae)

20 to 36 in.

July to October

Of the many, mostly perennial, species of centaurea growing wild in almost all parts of the world only a few are treated as annuals. Best known is *Centaurea cyanus* – the cornflower or blue bottle – which is an erect plant of thick bushy habit growing to a height of 20 to 36 in. and bearing a profusion of flowers. The flowerheads resemble those of the common cornflower of the fields but are double, resulting from a change in the form and enlargement of the central, tube-shaped florets. Most commonly grown are the blue-flowering forms but also cultivated are those with white, pink and red blooms. The flowering season is comparatively short – only about six weeks.

Centaurea moschata is a native of Asia Minor. The densely branched plants of spreading habit grow to a height of 2 to 2 1/2 ft. The fragrant flowerheads measure 2 to 2 1/2 in. across and are borne on long, firm stalks. They may be white, yellow, pink, deep as well as pale violet, and purple. Faded flowerheads should be removed promptly.

Centaurea flourishes in almost any soil with sufficient lime and in a warm, sunny position. The seeds should be sown outdoors where the plants are to flower, and not too deep. The spacing should be 10 to 16 in., depending on the variety. They will germinate within two weeks.

Centaurea is used primarily for cutting. The attractive, pastel-coloured flowers, which must be cut when partly open, will last 5 to 9 days in water. *C. cyanus* is used mainly in mixed beds.

Chrysanthemum carinatum
SCHOUSB.

Painted Lady

Asteraceae
(Compositae)

20 to 40 in.
July to October

The most commonly grown chrysanthemum is *Chrysanthemum carinatum*, the painted lady, from North America. It is a fairly delicate plant of spreading habit with many branching stems, growing to a height of 20 to 40 in. The leaves are twice divided, threadlike, and grey-green. The stems are fairly thick with few laterals and are topped by daisy-like flowers 2 1/2 to 3 in. across. The florets in the central boss are dark to blackish-purple, the outer, tongue-shaped petals are white, yellow, carmine to fiery red, sometimes with a dark patch at the base forming a distinct ring of colour round the central boss. There are numerous named varieties, for example 'Rainbow' mixture – 20 in., multicoloured petals; 'Pole Star' – 40 in., white with dark centre; double forms are also obtainable.

Chrysanthemum segetum, the corn marigold, a native of Europe and North Africa, is another popular plant. Only 20 in. high, it is richly branched and bears up to 80 flowers. It, too, has given rise to numerous varieties, the best known being 'Eldorado' – canary yellow with brown centre; and 'Evening Star' – golden yellow. Another species still offered occasionally is *C. coronarium* from southern Europe. It grows to a height of 40 in. and has smaller flowers, both single and double, about 1 1/2 in. across.

All three species have no special requirements but do best in loose, well-drained, even stony, soil. *C. carinatum* likes lime, *C. segetum* does better in soil that is poor in lime.

The seeds should be sown outdoors in April, in rows 12 to 16 in. apart and not very deep. Germination occurs within 2 to 3 weeks but is very unequal if the seeds are sown too deep. The seeds may also be sown in a frame and the seedlings planted in their flowering positions at the end of May. Faded flowers should be removed promptly.

Chrysanthemums are good for the mixed bed as well as the border but they are mainly used for cutting, the flowers lasting 7 to 13 days in water.

Chrysanthemum parthenium
(L.) PERS.

Syn. *Matricaria eximia* HORT.

Feverfew

Asteraceae
(Compositae)

8 to 28 in.

July to August

Chrysanthemum parthenium is a native of southern Europe and Asia Minor. It is a perennial but is treated as an annual, even though it will sometimes grow a number of years in the same site. Generally offered are the dwarf forms such as 'Golden Ball'. The 8-to 12-in.-high plants are of compact, densely branched habit and marked by a distinctive, penetrating fragrance. The leaves are regularly notched and coloured pale green, the small flowerheads, 3/4 to 1 in. across, are coloured bright yellow or white and when fully open completely conceal the leaves. The flowering period is fairly brief – from the beginning of July to the second half of August.

C. parthenium flourishes in ordinary garden soil with sufficient lime and in a warm, sunny position. The seeds should be sown in boxes at the end of February or beginning of March. Hardened-off seedlings should be moved to their outdoor places in mid-May.

C. parthenium is used for borders, edgings and in flowerpots. Because it transplants very well, fully grown plants can be removed from the bed and put in bowls or pots in various places for purposes of decoration.

Clarkia elegans DOUGL.

Oenotheraceae

1 1/2 to 2 ft.

June to August

Clarkia elegans is a native of California. It is a 1 1/2 to 2 ft. high plant of branching habit with blue-green, hoary leaves. Coloured forms have a reddish stem and a reddish mid-rib. The flowers are double, 1 to 1 1/2 in. across, white, pink, salmon, scarlet or purple. They are borne in the axils of the leaves in long, graceful spikes. The individual varieties are listed in seedsmen's catalogues according to colour, most popular being the mixed colours. The flowering season is fairly brief, lasting from the end of June till mid-August.

Clarkia flourishes in any garden soil and in a warm, sunny position sheltered from the wind. It is intolerant of soil that is excessively wet.

The seeds should be sown in April under glass, where they germinate within 10 days. The young seedlings must be pricked out or thinned in time and provided with ample ventilation, for otherwise they may easily grow tall and thin. In the middle of May the hardened-off seedlings may be moved to their flowering positions spaced 8 to 12 in. apart. However, plants sown outdoors in loose, damp soil often have a better growth than those sown under glass. In dry weather, of course, or when the soil cakes after the seeds have been sown germination is very unequal and often the seeds do not germinate at all. Plants will branch better if the growing point is pinched out once during the seedling stage.

Clarkia is planted singly in mixed beds as well as in separate groups. It is also very rewarding as a cut flower, lasting up to nine days in the vase. The stem should be cut as soon as the bottom-most flower opens. When growing clarkia for cutting it is best to set the plants out close together and to cut whole plants.

Cleome spinosa JACQ.

Capparidaceae

Syn. *Cleome pungens* WILD

Spider Flower

3 1/2 ft.

June to October

Of the many species that grow wild in South and North America the only one of use as an ornamental is *Cleome spinosa,* native to Mexico. Up to 3 1/2 ft. high, the plant is of spreading habit, branching broadly from the base. Clusters of flowers, that open in succession, develop at the top of the stems. A large number of long thin stamens, bearing purple anthers, project out and beyond the narrow, white, pink, carmine and deep mauve petals creating a spidery effect. Cleome bears continuous flowers from mid- June until the first frosts. The,available selection is not very large, that which is usually offered being 'Helen Campbell' – white, 'Pink Queen' – pink, 'Violet Queen' – violet, or a mixture of colours.

Cleome does best in sandy, well-drained soil and in a warm sunny position. The seeds should be sown during the month of May in boxes in the greenhouse or under glass. The young seedlings require a fair degree of heat. The best method of growing seedlings is in peat pots. After being hardened off they may be moved to their flowering positions, at least 20 in. apart, at the end of May.

Cleome is an annual still very little used, even though its habit of growth, foliage and profusion of airy flowers make it a very decorative plant. It is planted in large masses as well as singly in parks, public areas and also in mixed beds; it may be used alongside walls and fences.

Convolvulus tricolor L.

Convolvulaceae

8 to 12. in.

June to September

Of the many annual and perennial species distributed throughout the temperate and subtropical zones the one of importance for decorative purposes is *Convolvulus tricolor,* native to southern Europe and North Africa. It is a plant of richly branching, prostrate habit with only the tips of the branching stems growing vertically and forming around 12-in.-high bushes up to 30 in. across. The leaves are longish ovate. The funnel-shaped flowers, about 2 in. across, are brightly coloured and borne on short stalks. They grow in the axils of the leaves, which they conceal completely when in bloom. They are edged with blue, red or pink and the throat is yellow with an irregular margin. The flowering season extends from the end of June until autumn. One drawback of this annual is that the flowers close in dull or rainy weather; in fine weather they are open from seven o'clock in the morning until three in the afternoon.

Convolvulus flourishes in nourishing, warm, well-drained soil with sufficient lime and in a sunny situation. In poor soil it bears few flowers; in damp soil that is too rich the flowers are concealed by the lush growth of the foliage.

The seeds should be sown where the plants are to flower, 12 to 16 in. apart, in the month of April. They may also be sown under glass but only very young seedlings can be moved satisfactorily.

Convolvulus is used for mixed beds and as a quick-growing ground cover for large, empty spaces.

Coreopsis drummondii *Asteraceae*
(DON) TORR. and GRAY *(Compositae)*
Syn. *Coreopsis basalis* (DIETR.) BLAKE
Tickseed 1 1/2 to 2 ft.

June to October

Annual as well as perennial species grow wild in North and South America as well as in Africa. They exhibit marked differences in height and also in the size and shape of the leaves. Of the annuals most widely cultivated are the various forms of *Coreopsis tinctoria* (syn. *Calliopsis bicolor, Calliopsis tinctoria*), which is native to North America. The erect, greatly branching plants grow to a height of 3 ft. and bear a rich profusion of small, yelow, brownish-yellow to purplish-brown flowers. Tall forms produce flowers continuously throughout the summer, dwarf varieties flower for 5 to 6 weeks, during which time they form a magnificent brightly coloured carpet. Also cultivated, but to a lesser degree, is *Coreopsis basalis* of Texas. The plants are 1 1/2 to 2 ft. high, the branching stems not very sturdy and covered with a fine down. The flowers, up to 3 in. across and coloured a deep yellow with a brown central disc, bloom from July till the end of September.

Coreopsis does best in sandy, loamy soil and in a sunny position. Tall varieties, which are often much damaged by wind and rain when in full bloom, should be planted in a position sheltered from the wind.

The seeds should be sown under glass in April and the seedlings moved to their outdoor places (spaced 4 to 14 in. apart according to the variety) in the middle of May. The seeds may also be sown in the open where they are to grow at the end of April or beginning of May. If the faded flowers are removed promptly the plants will produce a second crop.

Low-growing varieties are used as border and edging plants and for mixed beds, where they are planted in smaller or larger clumps. Tall varieties are used for cutting. Closed flowers open in the vase and last for 8 to 10 days.

Cosmos bipinnatus CAV.

Cosmea

Asteraceae
(Compositae)

3 to 4 ft.

July to September

A number of annual and perennial *Cosmos* species grow wild in Mexico, Bolivia and the warm areas of North America.

Cosmos bipinnatus, a native of Mexico, is a plant of branching habit growing to a height of 3 to 4 ft. The leaves are a vivid green and delicately cut. The single flowers measure up to 4 in. across and come in bright glowing colours. They are offered both in separate as well as mixed colours: 'Radiance' – dark pink with purple centre, 'Sensation' – white, 'Sensation Gloria' – pale pink, 'Sensation Dazzler' – glowing carmine. Some catalogues also offer double varieties. *Cosmos sulphureus*, native of Mexico and Bolivia, is an erect, much branching plant of somewhat lower growth – 2 to 3 ft. The foliage is more coarsely cut and not as decorative as that of *C. bipinnatus*. The flowers are smaller, 1 1/2 to 2 in. across, but come in bright glowing shades of yellow to orange. Some forms are semi-double. Very attractive is the orange 'Sunset'. Both species of cosmos flower from July until late autumn.

Cosmos flourishes in any garden soil and in a warm, sunny position sheltered from the wind, for the mature plants are often damaged by strong winds when in full bloom. Excessively rich soil as well as too much shade causes the plants to bear few flowers.

The seeds should be sown under glass in March or April and the seedlings planted out at least 16 in. apart in the second half of May when there is no longer any danger of frost. The seeds may also be sown outdoors at the end of April but then flowering is much later.

Cosmea is grown mostly for cutting, the half-opened buds opening in the vase and lasting 7 to 8 days. It is also good in separate groups or as a hedge.

Crepis rubra L.

Hawkweed

Asteraceae
(Compositae)

16 in.

June to July

Crepis rubra is a native of southern Europe. The smooth, deep green, lyre-shaped leaves are arranged in a thick ground rosette from which emerge long smooth and firm stems. The double, dandelion-like heads of pale pink, tongue-shaped flowers with deeper centres measure about 1 in. across and close in the afternoon. Hawkweed flowers soon after sowing but only for a fairly brief period, the blooms fading within 4 weeks. The flowering season can be prolonged, however, by sowing the seeds in succession.

Crepis thrives in any garden soil and even in fairly poor soil, such as on building sites and in newly laid gardens. In unfenced country areas the plants should be provided with protection against hares.

The seeds should be sown outdoors where the plants are to flower, 8 to 12 in. apart, at the beginning of April. Crepis is used for mixed beds, for the rock garden and dry wall, on terraces and patios.

114

Cucurbita pepo ovifera L. (ALEF) *Cucurbitaceae*

Gourd

(Climber)

June to September

The gourd is generally known as a vegetable or farm crop but *Cucurbita pepo ovifera* is grown solely for ornament. The plant has up to 10-ft.-long creeping and climbing stems with strong tendrils. The large, up to 8-in.-wide, long-stalked leaves are palmately cut and hairy. The flowers are bell like and golden yellow but insignificant for purposes of decoration. Ornamental gourds are cultivated for their rapid growth, rich foliage and above all for the fruits of widely differing shape and colour, which are exceptionally good for winter decoration. The fruit is not edible but is a very interesting subject.

The gourd requires a nourishing, humus-rich soil and a warm, sunny position. During the growing period it should be watered and supplied with fertilisers according to need.

The seeds should be sown outdoors, best of all in pinches spaced 1 1/2 to 2 ft.apart, at the beginning of May. They may also be sown at the end of April in pots in a frame or greenhouse and the seedlings planted out at the end of May. Plants sown under glass and then moved outdoors have a more rapid rate of growth.

Cucurbita pepo is used for quickly covering larger areas, sun-facing slopes, compost heaps and the like. If it is to be used to mask walls or fences it should be provided with a support.

116

Cynoglossum amabile

Boraginaceae

STAFF and DRUMM.
Hound's Tongue

16 in.

June to August

Cynoglossum amabile from western China, though a biennial in its native habitat, is usually grown as an annual for garden decoration. It is a 16-in.-high plant with branching stems and long, rough, lance-shaped leaves, bearing numerous sprays of small, funnel-shaped, turquoise-blue flowers resembling large forget-me-nots. Other shades are nondescript. The flowering season begins in the middle of June and lasts until August.

The hound's tongue flourishes in light, nourishing soil with sufficient lime and in a warm, sunny situation. It does not thrive in very rich or heavy, wet soil.

The seeds should be sown in the open, spaced 8 to 12 in. apart, in the middle of April. They should not be sown too deep because then germination is very slow and unequal. If sown at the correct depth they will germinate within 10 days. Prompt removal of faded flowers will greatly prolong the flowering period. Cynoglossum sows itself freely so that the following year all that needs to be done is to thin the new seedlings and the bed will flower anew.

Cynoglossum is used for mixed borders or as a rapid ground cover of derelict areas in housing estates. When in full bloom it is a great attraction for bees.

Delphinium consolida L.

Ranunculaceae

Larkspur

1 1/4 to 4 1/4 ft.

June to July

A great many species of *Delphinium* grow as weeds in the Mediterranean, south-eastern Europe and Asia Minor. Many of them, both annual and perennial, are very attractive and very good for purposes of decoration. Most of the currently offered varieties of summer delphiniums have been developed from *D. consolida* and *D. ajacis*. They are divided into several groups according to height and size and shape of the flowers. Best known are the low-growing, hyacinth-flowered varieties – 16 to 20 in. high, producing thick flower spikes fairly early in the season and the giant hyacinth-flowered varieties – up to 3 1/2 ft. high.

Delphinium requires nourishing, well-drained soil and a warm, sunny, sheltered position, for tall varieties are often greatly damaged by wind during the flowering season.

The seeds should be sown in the open, spaced 5 to 10 in. apart, and not too deep, best of all in late autumn before the soil freezes or else as early as possible in spring. They may also be sown in succession. Germination is slow and takes 15 to 21 days. Seeds sown in the autumn flower in June, those sown in spring flower in July. The flowering season is 6 to 8 weeks.

Tall forms are used mostly for cutting and will last 5 to 7 days. They are very striking when whole plants are arranged in large vases. Low-growing forms are very nice in mixed beds, in groups as well as in larger areas in parks.

Dianthus barbatus L.

Sweet William

Silenaceae
(Caryophyllaceae)

10 to 24 in.

May to July

Dianthus barbatus is a biennial native to southern Europe. The broad, lance-shaped, dark green, short-stalked leaves form a clump from which emerge 10-to 24-in.-long stems bearing clusters of flowers at the top. Breeders have developed many varieties in single as well as mixed colours which are further divided according to height (low-growing, tall) and form of flower (single, double). The flowers are white or red and begin to bloom at the end of May, the flowering period being 5 to 8 weeks. Also available are varieties that are sown in March and flower in August to September of the same year.

Sweet Williams flourish in any good garden soil with sufficient lime and in a warm, sunny position. They are intolerant of fresh farmyard manure as a fertiliser.

The seeds should be sown at the end of May in a cold frame or seedbed raked to a fine tilth. Even though the plants will often grow in the same place for a number of years, Sweet William is usually grown as a biennial, newly sown and planted every year. Hardened-off seedlings are moved to their permanent positions, spaced 1 ft. apart, between mid-August and mid-September. The plants should be provided with a light cover of evergreen twigs as protection against frost and with some form of fencing to protect them from hares if these are likely to be a problem.

Sweet Williams are very popular for cutting because the flowers last long and stand up well to transportation. The various forms are also good as border and bedding plants and for planting in large or small groups.

Dianthus chinensis L.

Chinese or **Indian Pink**

Silenaceae
(Caryophyllaceae)

14 to 28 in.

July to October

The crossing of *Dianthus caryophyllus* (carnation) with many other species has yielded a vast number of varieties grown as annuals and biennials. The individual groups differ in the time of flowering, shape of flower, length of stem, and habit of growth. Seedsmen's catalogues list them all under *D. caryophyllus*. The most widespread are the Chabaud carnations – up to 20 in. high with double, pleasantly scented flowers measuring 2 1/4 in. across and borne on long, firm stems. They are treated as annuals, flowering from July until the autumn months.

The biennial types are hardy and bear a great profusion of flowers (one plant has up to 80, somewhat smaller than the type but pleasantly scented and all opening at one time). Only the double varieties are good for cutting. The flowering season is in June and July.

Grown as annuals are a great many forms of *D. chinensis*, the Chinese or Indian pink from China. The plants are delicate, branching, 6 to 16 in. high. The single and double flowers are 3 to 3 1/2 in. across, often multicoloured and unscented.

Biennial carnations should be sown in May to June and planted out in August. Annuals should be sown in January. *D. chinensis* varieties are sown in March and planted out in their permanent positions 12 to 16 in. apart (according to the variety) at the beginning of May.

Low-growing varieties are used for borders and mixed beds. They are also useful as cut flowers as they stand up well to transportation.

Didiscus coeruleus (GRAH.) DC.

Daucaceae
(Umbelliferae)

Syn. Trachymene coerulea GRAH.

2 ft.

Blue Lace Flower

July to October

The only species used for decoration is *Didiscus coeruleus* from western Australia. It grows to a height of 2 ft., is of sparse, irregular habit with a distinct main stem. The foliage is also thin. The bottom leaves are palmate and stalked, the top leaves tripartite and sessile. The sky-blue flowers with striking white anthers are borne in single, slightly rounded cymes. The stems are firm, up to 20 in. long and covered with a light down. One plant may have as many as 25 flowers. The flowering season is from mid-July until the beginning of October.

Didiscus does best in light, sandy loam and in a warm, sunny position. It is intolerant of wet soil and long rainy spells are detrimental to the plants.

The seeds should be sown at the beginning of March. Hardened-off seedlings should be moved to their outdoor places, spaced 8 to 12 in. apart, at the end of May. Young seedlings root better if they are first grown in pots.

Didiscus is planted in large as well as smaller groups in mixed borders. It may also be planted in earthenware urns or large pots or tubs and used for decoration. It is likewise good for cutting, especially for modern flower arrangements. The flowers may be cut when they first begin to bloom, in their prime and also when they have faded, the clusters of red fruits on their red stalks being very decorative, too.

Dimorphotheca sinuata DC.

Star of the Veldt

Asteraceae
(Compositae)

12 to 16 in.

June to September

The Star of the Veldt is a native of South Africa. The varieties offered nowadays are mostly hybrids resulting from the crossing of two species, *Dimorphotheca calendulacea* and *D. sinuata,* and generally listed under *D. aurantiaca.* The plants are of broadly spreading to prostrate habit. The stem and foliage are covered with small glandular hairs and when touched give off a strong scent. The leaves are elongate, sessile and irregularly lobed. The daisy-like flowers measure 2 1/4 to 4 in. across and are generally coloured golden-orange with a darker centre, though white forms are also available as well as a mixture of white, cream, yellow, orange and apricot-pink hues. One plant bears 25 to 40 flowers which close at night. The flowering period is from June to September. The best known forms are 'Glistening White', 'Tetra Goliath' and 'Orange Glory'.

Dimorphotheca thrives in dry, well-drained, sandy loam and in a warm, sunny situation. It is intolerant of wet soil.

It does not transplant well and therefore should be sown where it is to flower, but not too deep, at the end of April. The seedlings should be thinned to 8 to 10 in. between plants. Prompt removal of faded flowers will prolong the flowering period. The plants are also intolerant of long rainy spells.

Dimorphotheca is used for borders, mixed beds, dry walls and dry, sun-facing slopes. It is most effective when planted in large masses. In recent years breeders have developed forms bearing large flowers with a silky sheen on long stems that may also be used for cutting, as they do not close indoors.

Dorotheanthus bellidiformis *Aizoaceae*

(BURM) N. E. BR.

Syn. *Mesembryanthemum criniflorum*

(L.) SCHWANT.   4 in.

Livingstone Daisy   June to August

This pretty annual is a native of South Africa, where there are several known wild species. For purposes of decoration, however, the only one of any significance is *Dorotheanthus bellidiformis*. The plants are very small (4 in.), of spreading to prostrate habit, with reddish succulent stems and flat, elongate, succulent leaves. The single, wide-open flowers measure up to 2 in. across and are coloured whitish pink, salmon or deep carmine, always slightly paler round the centre, which is a darker colour with striking blue stamens. Dorotheanthus bears a profusion of flowers, as many as 120 on a single plant, which close at night and in dull weather. The flowering season lasts from the end of June until August. In seedsmen's catalogues it is offered in mixed colours.

Dorotheanthus thrives in dry, sandy soil and in a warm, sunny situation. It is intolerant of wet soil and lengthy periods of rain.

The seeds should be sown in a frame or in boxes at the end of April. Small pots are also very good. The young seedlings should be planted out 8 to 10 in. apart after all danger of frost is past.

This annual is very good for very dry sites, dry walls, dry sun-facing slopes or embankments, between paving stones or cement slabs in the patio, in the rock garden and also in earthenware urns.

Eschscholtzia californica CHAM. *Papaveraceae*

Californian Poppy

12 to 16 in.

June to October

Of the many, often perennial species widespread in the western United States, the only one of any significance is *Eschscholtzia californica* from California. It is a much-branched plant, 12 to 16 in. high, with very ornamental, finely cut foliage coloured silvery green. The single flowers measure 2 to 3 in. across and fade fairly quickly but new ones are continually opening so that the plant produces a profusion of blooms from mid-June till the autumn. Breeders have developed a great many varieties in glowing colours – pink, carmine, fiery red, yellow, orange and white. There are single, semi-double and double forms as well as ones with pretty fluted or ruffled petals. The flowers open only in sunny weather from ten o'clock in the morning till five in the afternoon.

The Californian poppy flourishes in dry, sandy soil and in a sunny situation. It does not like the application of too much fertiliser. Because it has a tap root, it does not transplant well and the seed should therefore be sown in the flowering positions from March onward. Seeds sown in the autumn also do well, producing flowers by the end of May. Seedlings must be thinned to 8 to 12 in. apart.

The Californian poppy is used for mixed beds, as an edging and border plant and also between newly planted perennials. It is very good in the new garden where, at comparatively little cost, one can have a flowering carpet the whole summer long. It also does well on sun-facing slopes and embankments.

Gaillardia pulchella FOUG.
Syn. *Gaillardia bicolor* LAM.
Blanket Flower

Asteraceae
(Compositae)

8 to 28 in.

July to October

Gaillardia is a native of Central and North America. *Gaillardia pulchella* is an annual of broad, branching habit and varied height, depending on the variety. The leaves are grey-green, rough, elongate and lobed. The flowers are borne on long firm stems and are generally bicolored, yellow and reddish-brown. In single forms the central disc is orange at first and later dark brown. Well-known varieties include 'Blood-red Giants'– a striking crimson strain, and 'Lollipops' – a cream, yellow and crimson mixture. Very ornamental are the double forms with globular flowerheads, up to 2 1/4 in. across, made up of tube-shaped, deeply cut flowers coloured pale to deep yellow or scarlet to brownish-red with a yellow border. They bloom from July until late autumn and are not damaged by mild frosts.

Gaillardia requires a well-drained, nourishing soil and a warm, sunny position. The plants often die in heavy, wet soil.

The seeds should be sown under glass from mid-March to the beginning of April and the hardened-off seedlings planted out 12 to 16 in. apart in the middle of May. Faded flowers should be removed promptly.

This species is very good in separate beds and borders as well as in a mixed bed. The double forms, in particular, always attract attention with their interesting blooms. One such plant may have as many as 50 very full blooms that are valuable as cut flowers for they last 5 to 8 days in water.

Gazania splendens MOORE

Treasure Flower

*Asteraceae
(Compositae)*

8 to 12 in.
June to October

Gazania is a native of South Africa, where a number of both perennial and annual species grow wild. Cross-breeding of several species has yielded numerous hybrids that are generally offered in a mixture under the title *G. splendens*. The plants are 8 to 12 in. high with a ground rosette of lance-shaped, sometimes shallowly lobed leaves that are smooth above and white-felted on the underside. The daisy-like flowers on firm and smooth but fairly delicate stems measure 2 1/2 to 3 1/2 in. across and come in a wide range of brilliant hues – white, straw yellow, deep yellow, orange to brown or bright red (the depth of colour of the brown and red hues changes during the flowering period), with a central disc of contrasting colour, usually dark, edged with a ring of darker hue with white and bluish spots. The flowering season extends from the end of June until late autumn. One drawback, however, is that the flowers do not open until about nine o'clock in the morning and close at about five in the afternoon.

Gazania requires nourishing, well-drained soil and a warm, sunny position, though the first mild frosts of autumn will not damage the flowers.

The seeds should be sown in boxes during the month of March. The seedlings transplant very readily and should be spaced 12 in. apart when moved to their permanent positions. They may be put out after bulbs or biennials have finished flowering.

Gazania is most striking when planted in large masses. It is good for edging, for mixed borders, sun-facing slopes, dry walls, boxes on balconies and larger earthenware urns.

Godetia grandiflora LINDL.
Syn. *Godetia whitneyi* HORT.

Oenotheraceae

8 to 16 in.

July to August

Godetia grandiflora is a native of America. The varieties offered today are generally hybrids of various, no-longer-known species. They are branching plants of compact habit and varied height. The gaily coloured flowers of many glowing hues measure 2 1/2 to 4 in. across. The various forms are classed either according to height (dwarf, intermediate, tall) or according to the form of the flower (single, double). Examples of single varieties are 'Sybil Sherwood' and 'Duke of York', double varieties – 'Double Kelvedon Glory', 'Pink Frills' and the Azalea-flow-ered sorts. The plants bear a great profusion of flowers which, when in their prime, completely hide the leaves. The flowering period is 4 to 6 weeks, beginning the end of June or early July.

Godetia thrives in any garden soil in a warm, sunny situation. It is intolerant of wet as well as excessively fertilised soil.

The seeds should be sown in the open or under glass in March. However, seedlings do not transplant readily. The seed must not be put at too great a depth when sowing outdoors. Germination will also be unequal if the soil forms a crust. Sometimes it is necessary to repeat the sowing. The spacing should be 8 to 16 in., depending on the variety. The flowering period may be prolonged by sowing in succession or nipping the young seedlings.

Godetia is used as a border plant and for mixed beds. It makes a magnificent display when planted in larger groups. Tall forms make graceful cut flowers. Though the blooms soon fade, practically all the buds will open in the vase.

Gypsophila elegans M. B.

Baby's Breath, Chalk Plant

Silenaceae
(Caryophyllaceae)

6 to 20 in.
June to July

Gypsophila is native to the eastern Mediterranean countries, Asia Minor and Central Asia. Most species are perennials and only a few are annuals. Of the latter only two are of importance as ornamentals. One is *Gypsophila elegans* from the Caucasus. This is a branching, slender plant of spreading habit, growing to a height of 20 in. with clouds of small, regular, 5-partite flowers measuring 3/4 in. across. The narrow, lance-shaped leaves resemble those of carnations. The flowers may be coloured white, pink or red, white varieties being the most common, for example 'Covent Garden White' and 'Paris Market White'. Also offered occasionally is the species *G. muralis* from Asia Minor. It resembles *G. elegans* but is only 4 to 6 in. high, with clouds of very small, pale purple or white flowers. Gypsophila has a fairly short flowering period, 4 to 5 weeks, beginning the end of June. This may be extended by sowing the seeds in succession.

Gypsophila flourishes in well-drained, sandy loam with sufficient lime and in a dry, sunny situation. It tolerates very dry periods, but decays when there is too much rain.

The seeds should be sown outdoors in their permanent places 8 to 12 in. apart in April. Low-growing forms are sown in rock gardens and dry walls. Tall forms are used for cutting and will last about 5 days in water.

Helianthus annuus L.

Sunflower

Asteraceae
(Compositae)

1 1/2 to 10 ft.

July to September

The sunflower is a native of America, which abounds in many annual as well as perennial species. Some annuals are good as ornamentals, for example *Helianthus annuus,* which has numerous forms divided into groups according to height and shape of flower. Offered in catalogues, for instance, are 'Autumn Beauty' – 7 ft. high, single, yellow to reddish-brown; 'Sungold' – 5 ft. high, double, yellow; and 'Dwarf Double Sungold' – 2 ft. high, double, golden-yellow. *H. debilis* (syn *H. cucumerifolius)* is another species of merit as an ornamental. It is shorter, more branching, and has smaller, finer leaves than *H. annuus.* The medium-sized blooms are yellow to brownish-red with large outer, tongue-shaped florets and a small, pronounced centre. The flowering period lasts from mid-July until autumn.

The sunflower thrives in any garden soil in a warm, sunny situation. It is intolerant of wet and cold soil. It requires ample nutrients if it is to grow and flower well. Compost should be added to the soil in good quantity in the autumn where the plants are to grow and artificial fertiliser applied several times during the growing period until the flowers appear. Water must also be applied in drought periods. Tall forms should be sown in situations sheltered from the wind and if necessary tied to a stake for support.

The seeds should be sown outdoors at the end of April, best of all in pinches spaced 16 to 28 in. apart. The seedlings should be thinned to one plant at each spacing.

Sunflowers are planted separately or in small clumps in mixed beds of tall plants, as solitary subjects or as a hedge, to mask walls and fences, and to demarcate or separate large areas. They are also good as cut flowers in large vases in shop windows, exhibition rooms and the like.

Helichrysum bracteatum
(VENT.) WILLD.

Strawflower

Asteraceae
(Compositae)

1 1/2 to 3 ft.

July to October

Of the many annual and perennial species of *Helichrysum*, the only one of merit as an ornamental is *H. bracteatum*, treated only as an annual but growing wild as a perennial in its native Australia. It is a slender, upright plant of branching habit with firm lateral stems up to 1 1/2 ft. long. The rounded heads of stiff incurved bracts arranged in several rows measure 2 to 3 in. across when fully open. The flowering season begins in July and lasts until late autumn, each plant bearing 15 to 30 flowers. The range of colours includes white, pink, red, purplish violet and golden brown. Seedsmen's catalogues list a great number of varieties usually only according to colour. As far as height is concerned they are divided into two groups: *monstrosum* – tall, 2 1/2 to 3 ft. and *nanum* – low-growing, 18 to 20 in.

Helichrysum flourishes in any good garden soil but does best in one with good drainage and in a sunny position sheltered from winds, which may uproot or damage the plants when they are in full bloom.

The seeds should be sown thinly under glass at the end of March or beginning of April. If sown too thickly the young seedlings tend to grow tall and decay. Hardened-off seedlings should not be planted out until the end of May and should be spaced 8 to 12 in. apart.

Dwarf varieties are good for mixed beds or borders. Tall forms are used mostly for drying for winter decoration. Flowers which are to be dried should be cut just before they open and tied in small bunches, which are then hung in a dark and well-ventilated room. Freshly cut flowers are also very decorative in a vase.

Helipterum roseum
(HOOK) BENTH.

Syn. *Acroclinium roseum* (HOOK)

Asteraceae
(Compositae)

1 1/2 to 2 ft.

June to September

These Australian everlastings grow both as annuals and perennials in their native land. Of merit as an ornamental is, first and foremost, the annual *Helipterum roseum*. Breeding has produced several forms coloured white, pink or red; they are generally offered, however, in mixed colours. Some are double varieties with a greater number of incurved bracts, such as *H. plenum*. The plants branch densely, close above the ground and have lovely fresh green foliage that makes them an ornamental subject even before they flower. The leaves are narrow and sessile, the stems are up to 16 in. long and the flowerheads 1 1/2 to 2 in. across.

Helipterum manglesii is pink or white, about 12 in. high, with many branching stems. The small nodding flowerheads are borne on thin firm stalks.

Both species require a well-drained, humus-rich soil, preferably acid, and a warm sunny position. They do not tolerate soil with too much lime.

The seeds should be sown in a frame or in boxes at the end of March. Hardened-off seedlings, which transplant readily but must not be allowed to grow too tall, should be put outdoors in their flowering positions in the second half of May. They should be fenced in if there is any likelihood of hares and rabbits reaching them, otherwise they may be so nibbled within the space of a few days that they will not bear flowers.

These everlasting flowers are good in freshly cut flower arrangements as well as for drying. Partly opened flowers are tied in small bunches and hung upside down to dry in a dark, well-ventilated room. They are very good as winter decoration together with other dried flowers and ornamental grasses.

Iberis umbellata L.

Globe Candytuft

Brassicaceae
(Cruciferae)

1 ft.
June to July

Iberis amara, the rocket candytuft, grows as a wild plant in southern Europe. The hyacinth-flowered 'White Spiral' variety is of firm, erect habit with thickish, shallowly and irregularly toothed leaves, bearing fragrant white flowers in clusters which, as they mature, lengthen into spikes up to 4 in. long. A single plant bears 6 to 9 spikes. *I. umbellata,* the globe candytuft, also from southern Europe, forms a firm, semi-spherical, branching bush about 1 ft. high and the same across. The leaves are narrow and slender-pointed. The flowers are borne in thick clusters that do not lengthen into spikes. In full bloom the plant is completely covered with flowers. The colour range is white, pink, carmine, pale violet and purplish-violet. It is usually offered in mixed colours. The flowering period is brief – from the beginning of June to mid-July.

Iberis does best in sandy loam and in a warm, sunny situation. The seeds should be sown outdoors where the plants are to flower in early spring or else in a frame in March, the seedlings being planted in their permanent positions, 8 to 12 in. apart, in mid-May. Plants sown in their outdoor places should be thinned in time.

Iberis is good for mixed beds, in boxes, earthenware urns and in flower pots. It is very attractive when planted in large masses or groups. It is also excellent for cutting, lasting 7 to 10 days in water.

Impatiens balsamina L.   *Balsaminaceae*

Syn. *Balsamina hortensis* DC.

Balsam, Touch-me-not   8 to 24 in.

June to September

Impatiens balsamina is a native of eastern India. The plants are 8 to 24 in. high and have thick, fleshy stems, usually reddish, with distinct swollen nodes. The leaves are smooth and sessile. The large flowers are borne on short stalks in the axils of the leaves. They are both single and double, and coloured white, yellow, red or purple. The varieties are divided into various groups according to height and form of flower, for example camellia-flowered, rose-flowered, and the like.

Impatiens roylei (syn. *I. glandulifera)*, from the Himalayas, has thick fleshy stems reminiscent of the bamboo and grows to a height of 6 to 8 ft. The salmon, purple or wine-red flowers measure 1 to 1 1/2 in. across, and are arranged in loose panicles. *Impatiens holstii*, originally grown as a greenhouse plant but now treated more frequently as an annual, is a foot-high plant of spreading habit bearing a great profusion of flowers, especially the F_1 hybrids.

I. balsamina and *I. roylei* require good rich soil and a warm, sunny situation. *I. holstii*, on the other hand, does better in semi-shade. During the growth period fertiliser should be applied as needed.

I. balsamina and *I. holstii* should be sown into boxes in March and moved to their outdoor places, 8 to 14 in. apart, at the end of May. *I. roylei* is sown where it is to flower, 8 to 14 in. apart, at the end of April. All three species are very sensitive to frost.

Low-growing forms are good as border and edging plants as well as for balcony boxes. Intermediate and tall forms are good for mixed beds, in separate groups, and to mask walls and fences. *I. holstii* flowers well in boxes on the northern or eastern sides of buildings.

Ipomoea tricolor CAV.

Convolvulaceae

Syn. *Pharbitis rubro-caerulea* CHOISY

Morning Glory

7 to 16 ft.

June to September

Of the many species of *Ipomoea* that are generally perennials in the tropical regions of America, some are popularly grown as twining annuals. All are much alike and are distinguished by rapid growth and profuse flowering, the flowering season lasting from June until autumn and the arrival of frosts. The various forms of *Ipomoea nil* (syn. *Pharbitis nil*) are perennials but are treated as annuals, bearing blue, violet, rose and purple flowers that measure 2 to 3 in. across. The species *I. purpurea* (syn. *Pharbitis purpurea*) is the least demanding of all and is generally offered in mixed colours. The flowers open at dawn and last only 9 to 10 hours (longer in dull weather).

The loveliest forms, however, are those that have been developed from *I. tricolor*. The large, trumpet-shaped flowers, measuring 3 to 4 in. across, come in several colours with a white throat and sometimes also a white margin. Some forms change colour during the day – from red to sky blue. The flowers open in succession, 3 to 5 on a stalk. The best known forms are 'Heavenly Blue', 'Flying Saucers' and 'Scarlet O'Hara'.

Morning Glory requires a warm, sunny and sheltered situation but thrives in any garden soil. It is sensitive to cold weather (only *I. purpurea* is somewhat hardier).

Ipomoea purpurea should be sown outdoors where it is to flower, about 12 in. apart, in April or May. The other species should be sown in a frame in March or April, grown and hardened off in pots and planted in their permanent positions at the end of May.

Ipomoea is good planting in boxes and for covering pergolas, walls and fences. It grows very quickly and covers a large area within a very short time, but it must be provided with support.

Kochia scoparia trichophylla (VOSS) BOOM.

Chenopodiaceae

Summer Cypress, Fire Bush   32 to 40 in.

The only species of *Kochia* suitable for garden decoration is *K. scoparia,* native to south eastern Europe and Asia, which is grown for its ornamental habit and fine-cut foliage. The flowers are insignificant. It is a fast-growing, densely branched plant of neat, upright habit reaching a height of 32 to 40 in. The foliage is very thick, the leaves narrow, the colouring fresh green. There are two forms: *K. s. trichophylla,* that turns a lustrous red in the autumn, and *K. s. childsii,* that retains its fresh green colouring the whole season.

Kochia flourishes in any garden soil with sufficient nutrients and in a warm, sunny position. It may also be sown in poorer, neglected soil in housing developments, where it will grow nicely with subsequent applications of fertilisers and adequate watering, even though it will not attain the same proportions as under ideal conditions. It seeds itself quite freely and plenty of new seedlings will be found growing in the same place the following year.

Seeds should be sown outdoors in April, 16 to 32 in. apart. The seedlings transplant readily and can therefore be grown under glass in pots and used as replacements or else planted out when the final touches are being made to the garden layout.

Kochia is used to separate or demarcate beds and to mask walls and fences. As a hedge it stands up well to trimming and clipping. It may be planted singly, in small or large groups in grass, in front of houses and also in flower beds. It is very good for the decoration of public areas, and also in earthenware urns. It may also be taken up with the root ball, put in large pots and used as inexpensive, short-term decoration.

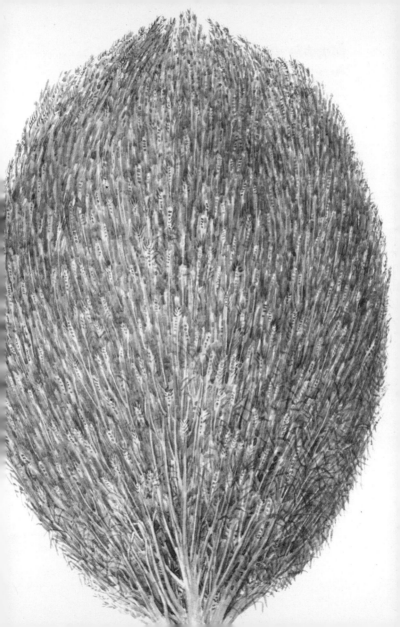

Lagurus ovatus L.

Hare's-tail Grass

Poaceae
(Gramineae)

8 to 16 in.

July to September

Lagurus ovatus, the only species of this genus, is native to the Mediterranean. It is covered with soft down and has flat leaves. The firm stems growing in thick clumps are topped by ovate to longish cylindrical spikes with long silky hairs. At first these are whitish-green, later turning pale grey. The flowering period is from July to September and can be prolonged by the time of sowing and by clipping the plants. There may be as many as 35 spikes to one plant.

Lagurus flourishes in any garden soil in a sunny position. The seeds should be sown in a frame in April and the hardened-off seedlings put out in their permanent positions, 12 in. apart, in the middle of May. The seeds may also be sown in the open but then the plants flower later.

Lagurus is used mainly for cutting for decoration, both fresh and dried. It is very attractive as winter decoration together with other everlasting plants. It may also be planted out by itself in small groups.

Lathyrus odoratus L.

Viciaceae
(Leguminosae)

Sweet Pea

1 to 5 ft.

June to August

Lathyrus odoratus, a native of southern Italy and Sicily, is an annual climber that grows to a height of 3 1/2 to 5 ft. and requires a support. A vast number of varieties have sprung from the original species. Present-day forms produce 4 to 8 large, fragrant flowers, in all colours except yellow, to each long, firm stem. Breeders have also produced low-growing (12 to 20 in. high), profusely flowering forms that do not require a support. The varieties are divided into several groups according to height, flowering period, and size and wealth of flowers, and in each group they are offered in 10 to 15 different colours. The flowering season varies, being determined by the time of sowing, the weather and by the nourishment the plant has. Plants sown in April begin to flower in mid-June and bear flowers over a period of about two months.

Sweet peas require a medium heavy, nourishing and well-drained soil and a warm, sunny situation.

The seeds should be sown where the plants are to flower at the end of March or beginning of April. The best support is a thin netting which can be used for a number of years. Earlier flowering may be obtained by growing seedlings in pots. If seeds are sown in succession it is possible to have flowers the whole summer long. However, it is also necessary to remove faded blooms promptly for as soon as the seed begins to ripen the plants quickly cease to flower.

The sweet pea is used to cover pergolas, fences and railings and it may also be planted in boxes. Its chief use is for cutting. One plant can produce over a hundred flowers that will last 4 to 6 days in water.

Limonium suworowii

O. KUNTZE

Plumbaginaceae

Syn. *Statice suworowii* REG.

1 1/2 to 3 ft.

Sea Lavender, Statice

July to August

Limonium suworowii is from Turkestan. It grows to a height of 1 1/2 to 3 ft. and has pale green leaves with wavy margins and up to 14-in.-long dense spikes of rose-pink flowers, sometimes known as pink pokers. The flowers are borne from July until the end of August.

Limonium bonduellii (syn. *Statice bonduellii*) is a native of North Africa. It forms a ground rosette of lyre-shaped leaves, from which rise branching, ribbed stems bearing compound flower clusters up to 2 1/4 in. long. The deciduous flowers and persistent calyx are yellow. *L. sinuatum* (syn. *Statice sinuata*) is from the Mediterranean, where it grows as a biennial or perennial. However, it is usually treated as an annual. The leaves are rough and leathery, and the much-branched, wing-like stems grow to a height of 3 ft. The flowers are much larger and more closely spaced than those of *I bonduellii* and are borne from July until the autumn. The deciduous corolla is white, the persistent calyx blue-violet, rose-violet or white. This plant is a favourite for cutting and may be dried as an 'everlasting', but the bright colouring of some hues fades and becomes dulled and greyish.

Limonium does best in warm, well-drained loamy soil that is not too heavy and has sufficient lime. It likes a sunny position, and is intolerant of fresh farmyard manure.

The seeds should be sown in a frame at the beginning of March. To be certain of good germination it is a good idea to soak the seeds before sowing. *L. suworowii* should be planted out 12 in. apart, the other species 16 in. apart, at the beginning of May.

Limonium is used primarily for drying as an everlasting for winter decoration and also for cutting. *L. suworowii* is also good in mixed beds.

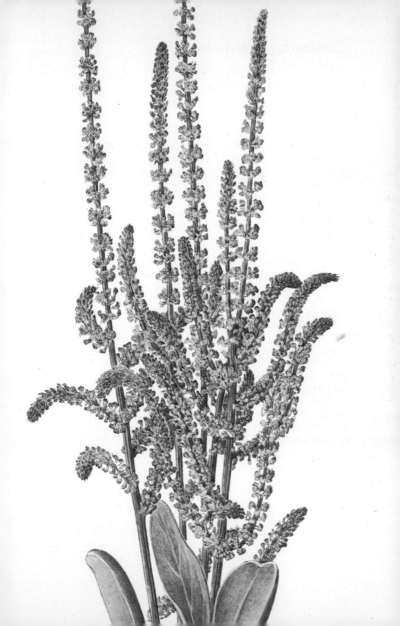

Linaria bipartita WILLD.

Scrophulariaceae

Toadflax

8 to 16 in.

June to August

A large number of annual as well as perennial species of this plant are widely distributed throughout Europe. Present-day forms are usually multiple hybrids of several species. The individual varieties are offered either in single colours (white, pink, red, yellow and violet) or mixed colours. Some even have bicolored flowers. The toadflax is an erect, densely branched plant of bushy habit. The narrow linear leaves are sessile and coloured pale green. The small, brightly coloured flowers resemble miniature snapdragons and are borne in great profusion. The flowering season is fairly short – from mid-June to mid-August for plants sown in April – but if cut back with shears after the first flush of flowers, a second crop will appear in the autumn.

Linaria has no special requirements and flourishes in any garden soil and in a warm, sunny position. Since it does not transplant well, the seeds should be sown outdoors where it is to flower, either in pinches or broadcast, between the beginning of March and middle of May. The flowering period may be prolonged by sowing the seeds in succession. Because they are very small the seeds should not be covered with soil but merely pressed in the ground. If sown too deeply they may not germinate. Thin the seedlings if they are overcrowded, but not necessarily to one plant; they may be left in small clumps of several seedlings which later form a thick and brightly coloured patch of blooms.

Toadflax is used for dry walls, mixed beds and to fill empty spaces in the rock garden. When sown in separate borders it forms an attractive and brightly coloured carpet.

Linum grandiflorum DESF.

Linaceae

Scarlet Flax

1 ft.

July to September

The only species of garden merit as an annual is *Linum grandiflorum* from North Africa. It is a plant of loose, profusely branching habit with small, bright green, lance-shaped leaves which make groups of these plants look very attractive even before they flower. The wide-open flowers, about 1 1/2 in. across, are coloured a bright red (*rubrum*) or white (*album*) with a dark centre. Though they do not las very long new ones appear in rapid succession, as many as 400 to a plant, so that there is a profusion of blooms throughout the summer from the beginning of July onward.

Linum has no special requirements and will grow in any garden soil in a warm, sunny position. The seeds should be sown in April in the open, either in pinches or broadcast, and the young seedlings thinned so that the plants are spaced some 8 in. apart.

The scarlet flax is good for mixed beds as well as for larger spaces. The brilliant splash of scarlet is striking even from a distance. It is also good, and fairly inexpensive, as a temporary ground cover in parks and housing developments before more permanent plants are put out.

Lobelia erinus L.

Campanulaceae

4 to 10 in.

June to September

Of the many species of the genus *Lobelia*, that of greatest merit is *L. erinus* from South Africa, which, though a perennial, is treated as an annual. It forms a compact, semi-spherical bush thickly covered with long, shallowly toothed leaves. Though varieties are available in white ('Snowball') as well as carmine-red ('Rosamond'), it is the blue-flowered ones that are the most popular, for example 'Crystal Palace', 'Cambridge Blue', 'Blue Stone' and 'Sapphire'. They usually begin to flower while still in the frame or shortly after being planted out and produce flowers the whole summer. The flowering period may be prolonged until autumn by clipping the plant when most of the flowers have faded. Plants are killed by the first autumn frost.

Lobelia does best in light, well-drained soil in a sunny situation. Trailing varieties tolerate semi-shade. In soil that is excessively rich or too wet growth is poorer and fewer blossoms are produced.

The seeds should be sown in boxes in February or March. They are very small and therefore need not be covered with soil. The young seedlings are quite small and are usually pricked out in clumps of 2 or 3. Lobelias are intolerant of frost and for that reason should not be planted out until the end of May (spaced 6 to 8 in. apart). They transplant well and can thus be grown in large pots and planted outdoors when fully grown and in full bloom.

Lobelias are good as edging plants, in separate low borders, in groups as bedding plants and for decoration in urns. The trailing varieties may be used in hanging baskets or in boxes on the balcony or patio.

Lobularia maritima (L.) DESV.

Syn. *Alyssum maritimum* LAM.

Sweet Alyssum

Brassicaceae

(Cruciferae)

3 to 10 in.

May to October

Lobularia maritima is a native of the Mediterranean. It forms a dense, flat-topped, spherical bush 6 to 10 in. high, bearing a great profusion of small, fragrant flowers that open in succession, completely covering the small, narrow, lance-shaped leaves. Most widely cultivated varieties are 'Little Dorrit', white, 3 to 4 in. high, and 'Rosie O'Day,' pink, also 3 to 4 in. high. In the later stages of growth the compact, semi-spherical plants are of more spreading habit, measuring as much as 10 to 14 in. across. They flower from the middle of May until late autumn.

Sweet alyssum flourishes in any garden soil in a warm, sunny situation. In excessively rich soil the plants grow tall and thin and bear fewer flowers.

The seeds should be sown outdoors in pinches or broadcast in early spring. Seedlings should be thinned to a spacing of about 6 in. The seeds may also be sown under glass and the hardened-off seedlings planted in their flowering positions in mid-May. Sweet alyssum transplants very well and can therefore be grown in pots and planted out when fully grown and in full bloom in spots made vacant by the removal of previously flowering bulbs or biennials.

Sweet alyssum is useful as an edging plant, for the rock garden and dry wall and also in boxes. It is sown under roses or amidst gladioli, on sunny slopes, and is also used as a rapid ground cover for unsightly areas. The flowers are a great attraction to bees.

Lonas inodora GAERTN.

Asteraceae
(Compositae)
12 to 16 in.
July to October

Lonas inodora is a native of the Mediterranean region. An annual of broadly branching habit, it has firm, reddish stems bearing a profusion of flowers. The leaves are long, deeply cut and covered with a fine down. The small, dark yellow, tube-shaped flowers are produced in clusters and bloom from mid-July until late autumn. The plants are not damaged by mild autumn frosts. Only the one form is offered under its botanical name.

Lonas has no special requirements and thrives in any garden soil in a sunny position. It is intolerant of excessive damp. The seeds should be sown under glass in March and the seedlings planted out, 10 to 14 in. apart, in the middle of May.

Because of its long flowering period and bright yellow colouring, lonas is very good for planting in small or large groups in the mixed border. It is also good for separating or marking out beds. If cut in time, the flowers can be dried in the same way as helichrysum. When dried in a dark and dry room they will retain their bright yellow colouring and may be used for winter decoration together with other everlastings.

Malope trifida CAV.

Malvaceae

2 to 3 ft.

July to October

Malope trifida is native to the Mediterranean region but nowadays grows wild in many central European countries. A plant of broadly spreading habit, it forms a large bush covered with large, rich green, palmately heart-shaped leaves. Popularly grown are the various forms of the variety *grandiflora* with broad, trumpet-shaped flowers up to 4 in. across, which open in succession from the bottom up. The colours are white, rose and purplish-red with darker venation. Malope is usually offered as a mixture, separate colours being available only occasionally. The flowering season is from the beginning of July till late autumn.

Malope does best in nourishing, sandy loam, rich in humus, and in a sunny situation. It will also grow in poorer soil but the plants are then not as large, though just as attractive.

Malope is noted for its ease of cultivation. The seeds should be sown in the open in pinches, 16 to 20 in. apart, in April. The seedlings should be thinned to two plants at the most. The seeds may also be sown in a frame, best of all in pots. The seedlings require liberal application of water during long drought periods.

Its large size makes malope a very good subject for planting singly in grass and for rapidly filling in empty spaces between tall perennials and woody plants. It is also very good for masking walls and fences and for demarcating large flower beds. Cut flowers last 6 to 8 days in water and single blooms are very attractive for table decoration.

Matthiola incana annua
(L.) R. BR.

Stock

Brassicaceae

(Cruciferae)

10 to 28 in.
June to July

Matthiola incana grows wild in the Mediterranean both as an annual and a short-lived perennial, the plants being either single-stemmed or branching, and growing to a height of 10 to 28 in. The long, finely felted leaves are coloured grey-green. The flowers, either single or double, have a penetrating scent. Double flowers measure 1 3/4 in. across and are arranged in spikes that gradually become longer. The colour range is quite extensive, only deep yellow and blue being absent. Only the double forms are good as ornamentals. The single plants are easily identified by the colour of the seed leaf (the dark green are single forms and the light green are doubles) and can be removed and discarded when pricking out the seedlings. The many forms are divided into various groups according to height, the time of flowering and the size of the flowers. The flowering season begins in June, with some forms bearing flowers until autumn.

Stocks do best in rich, sandy loam and in a warm, sunny position.

The seeds should be sown in early February. Because stocks have a tap root it is best to grow the seedlings in peat pots and plant them out in their flowering positions, 6 to 10 in. apart, from the beginning of April onward.

Low-growing and intermediate forms are best planted in separate borders in front of buildings or in smaller groups in grass. Taller forms are useful as cut flowers, especially in early summer when blooms for cutting are few.

Mimulus luteus L.

Monkey Flower

Scrophulariaceae

10 to 12 in.

June to September

Of the many species of this genus the one of merit as an ornamental annual is *Mimulus luteus*. In its native Chile it is a perennial and in central Europe will live a number of years in a sheltered position; however, it is usually treated as an annual because it flowers best the first year. The forms offered nowadays are low, branching bushes of broadly spreading habit. The leaves are egg-shaped, shallowly toothed and coloured bright green. The symmetrical, large, trumpet-shaped flowers measure 1 1/2 to 2 1/4 in. across and are borne on fairly long stalks in the axils of the leaves. The corolla has five sections and is bright yellow with red markings and blotches. As many as 150 blooms are borne in succession throughout the summer, beginning in early June.

Mimulus does best in moist, sandy loam rich in humus. It does not do well in a situation that is excessively wet or too dry. Unlike most annuals it grows well even in semi-shade.

The seeds should be sown in a frame or in boxes at the beginning of April. They are very tiny and should not be covered with soil but merely pressed in. More rapid branching of the seedlings may be achieved by pinching out the growing point. Hardened-off seedlings should be planted out 10 to 14 in. apart in mid-May. The monkey flower transplants fairly well and seedlings grown in pots can therefore be moved when in full bloom and planted in place of earlier-flowering species.

The monkey flower is used for balcony boxes, terraces, earthenware urns and low borders. It is most effective planted separately and in a position where its unusual flowers can be seen to good advantage.

Mirabilis jalapa L.

Mirabiliaceae
(Nyctaginaceae)

Marvel of Peru

2 to 2 1/2 ft.

July to October

Mirabilis jalapa is a native of Mexico, where it is a perennial, but it may also be treated as a half-hardy annual. The black, tuberous, beet-like roots can be stored for the winter the same as dahlia tubers and planted out in spring. Mirabilis makes an erect, rounded bush of broadly spreading habit thickly covered with leaves. The single trumpet-shaped flowers are white, yellow, rose, red and sometimes even bicolored. They open in the late afternoon and close again in the morning. The flowering season begins in July and lasts until late autumn, when the plants are killed by frost.

Mirabilis flourishes in deep, loamy soil and in a sunny position. It can also be grown in poorer soil but the plants are much thinner and should therefore be planted closer together.

The seeds should be sown thinly in rows in a frame in April. The young seedlings grow very fast and if sown thickly are inclined to grow tall and thin with a poor root system. They should be planted in their flowering quarters 16 to 20 in. apart at the end of May when all danger of frost is past.

Even when the flowers are closed the lush dark green foliage makes this a very attractive ornamental. It is planted singly or in larger groups alongside buildings, in grass as well as in beds. It is a good backdrop for low-growing flowers and its fast growth makes it eminently suitable for covering large, new areas.

Myosotis alpestris SCHMIDT

Forget-me-not

Boraginaceae

5 to 16 in.

April to May

Of the many different species of *Myosotis* the most important is *M. alpestris,* which grows wild throughout Europe, Siberia and the Orient and from which most of the developed types treated as biennials have sprung. The plants form thickly branched bushy shrubs of varying height. The dark green leaves and stems are lightly felted. The tiny flowers, 1/4 to 1/3 in. across and arranged in clusters, are generally blue, but there are also pink and white forms. The plants flower in April to May for a fairly brief period of about 3 to 4 weeks, depending on the weather.

Forget-me-nots do best in moist, humus-rich soil and in a sunny position, though they also stand up well to semi-shade. Excessive heat and insufficient moisture greatly shorten the flowering period.

The seeds should be sown in a cool greenhouse or well prepared seedbed in June. They should be shaded and kept moist, for if allowed to become too dry germination is unequal or the seeds may even not germinate at all. If sown thinly the seedlings need not be pricked out. August or early September is when they should be moved to a nursery bed for the winter, the plants spaced 6 to 8 in. apart, depending on the variety. Then in spring, either before they flower or else when already in bloom, they should be transferred to their permanent quarters.

Even though forget-me-nots flower for such a brief period, their early flowering and lovely blue colour make them great favourite as bedding plants.

Nemesia strumosa BENTH.

Scrophulariaceae

8 to 14 in.

June to September

The two species of garden merit are *Nemesia strumosa* and *N. versicolor*, the latter bearing flowers with a long spur. Both are annuals and both are natives of South Africa. Nemesia is an erect, thickly branching plant growing to a height of 8 to 14 in. and bearing a great profusion of flowers. Most of the large-flowered, coloured forms are descended from *N. strumosa*; the small-flowered and as a rule blue forms from *N. versicolor*. In seedsmen's catalogues they are often listed together as *Nemesia hybrida*. Best known varieties are *nana compacta*– white, orange, carmine; 'Aurora' – red and white; and the mixtures *suttonii*, 'Triumph' and 'Carnival'. The flowering period is from June to mid-August. If faded flowers are removed promptly the plants put out new shoots and flower until the first autumn frosts.

Nemesia thrives in light, well-drained soil in a warm, sunny situation. It is intolerant of excessive damp and is damaged by rain.

The seeds should be sown in a frame or in boxes in March or the beginning of April. If thinly sown the seedlings need not be pricked out. Hardened-off seedlings are moved to their flowering positions, spaced 8 in. apart, at the end of May when there is no longer any danger of frost.

Because of the brilliant, glowing colours and long flowering period nemesia is very good for the mixed bed and border as well as for planting separately in large masses or in groups. It is also attractive in the rock garden and dry wall as well as in balcony boxes and earthenware urns. Nemesia transplants well and thus mature plants may be removed with the root ball and put in flower pots. Cut flowers last a long time in water.

Nicotiana alata LINK and OTTO

Tobacco Plant

Solanaceae

16 to 32 in.

July to September

The tobacco plant is a native of the tropical regions of South America. Generally cultivated are *Nicotiana alata* and its variety *grandiflora* (syn. *N. affinis*). These grow to a height of 16 to 32 in. and bear large, funnel-shaped flowers with a very pleasant scent, coloured white with a greenish tint and violet stripes on the outside. There are also pink and red varieties. Also listed in catalogues is *N. sanderae* 'Scarlet King'.

Nicotiana is an erect plant of broadly branching habit reaching a height of 40 in. The leaves are of varying size, slightly glandular and coloured a bright green. The long, funnel-shaped, five-pointed corolla measures 2 in. across at the mouth. There are as many as 200 flowers to a plant; these open in the evening, though some forms remain open all day. The flowering season is from the beginning of July until autumn when the plants are killed by frost.

Nicotiana thrives in nourishing, loamy, humus-rich soil with good drainage and in a warm, sunny situation. It tolerates semi-shade.

The seeds should be sown in a frame in March or early April. The seedlings must be pricked out thinly before they become overcrowded or else grown in pots. They should be planted outdoors in beds (spaced 16 to 20 in. apart) after all risk of frost is past.

Low-growing varieties are attractive when planted singly in mixed flower beds; taller forms in separate groups, alongside buildings or in grass, to mask walls and fences. When used as cut flowers, buds open successively in the vase and emit a pleasant scent.

Nigella damascena L.

Ranunculaceae

Love-in-a-mist

16 to 20 in.

July to August

Nigella damascena grows wild in southern Europe and North Africa. It is an erect, much-branched plant, thickly covered with rich green, finely cut leaves. The light, airy plants with their dainty foliage are very attractive even before the flowers arrive. The latter are actually deciduous sepals coloured like petals, but it is the filament-like bracts surrounding them that are the plant's greatest attraction. The colours are blue, pale or deep pink as well as white. The flowers measure 1 1/2 in. across and there are as many as 120 to a single plant. The flowering season is fairly short but may be prolonged by sowing the seeds in succession. Plants sown in April begin to bear flowers in mid-July and finish flowering during the month of August. The ripening seed pods, however, make them attractive even after the flowers have faded. Best known are 'Miss Jekyll' – cornflower blue or white, and 'Persian Jewels' – a mixture.

Love-in-a-mist has no special requirements and thrives in any ordinary garden soil. Only excessively wet soil and too much rain have a detrimental effect on its growth.

The seeds should be sown in the open in pinches spaced 8 to 10 in. apart. They may also be sown under glass but this is not generally recommended for the seedlings do not transplant readily. Seedlings should eventually be thinned to two plants.

Love-in-a-mist is used for mixed beds grown from seeds sown in the open, also separately in smaller borders or small groups. When cut, fully open flowers will last 4 to 6 days in water. Ripe seed pods are very effective in modern floral arrangements.

Panicum capillare L.

Poaceae
(Gramineae)

Millet   2 ft.

July to September

Panicum capillare is native to North America. It is a grass of broadly branching habit. The leaves are almost linear and covered with down. The flowers are borne in pyramidal panicles 16 in. long and up to 3/4 in. wide. The separate stems of the panicle are rigid and jut outward. The main flowering season is July to September.

Panicum has no special requirements and thrives in any garden soil and in a warm, sunny situation. The seeds should be sown in a frame at the end of March or the beginning of April. The seedlings may be pricked out in clumps of 3 to 4. Hardened-off seedlings should be moved to their outdoor positions, 12 to 16 in. apart, in mid-May. Seeds may also be sown in the open but germination is sometimes very poor, it often being necessary to sow a second time, and for that reason sowing under glass is a more reliable method.

The plants are very decorative and are planted either separately in small or large groups or else in mixed beds. Millet is very good for cutting and can also be dried for winter decoration together with everlastings.

Papaver somniferum L.

Papaveraceae

Opium Poppy

1 to 4 ft.

June to July

The genus *Papaver* is very large and some of its members have been grown as garden ornamentals for several centuries. Many fine varieties with lovely blooms in bright glowing colours, though with a short flowering period, have been raised from the annual as well as biennial species. *Papaver glaucum* is from Asia Minor. It is 20 in. high with large, saucer-shaped flowers coloured a bright scarlet and borne in July and August. *P. rhoeas,* the corn poppy, is native to central Europe and grows to a height of 1 to 3 ft. The small-flowered varieties are grown only occasionally nowadays but the large-flowered singles and doubles are listed in every seedsman's catalogue. Usually offered is a mixture of white and various shades of red listed as 'Shirley' poppies. They flower in May to August, depending on the time of sowing.

P. somniferum embraces varieties that differ widely in height (1 to 4 ft.) and form of flower, including peony-flowered (both single and double with wavy, entire or only slightly notched margins) and carnation-flowered (double with delicately cut to feathery petals) in many different colours excepting yellow and blue. The flowering period is June and July.

Widely grown as a biennial is *P. nudicaule,* the Iceland poppy, which is sown in June or July. It bears flowers for quite a lengthy period the following year from June to August and the blooms last longer than those of *P. somniferum.*

Plants do best in loose, loamy, nourishing soil with sufficient lime. The seeds of the annual types should be sown directly in the open ground in early spring. The plants make a tap root and do not tolerate transplanting. Seedlings should be thinned in time to at least 4 to 6 in. apart.

The poppy is useful for mixed beds and as a rapid cover for empty spaces. Cut flowers are very attractive but last only a very short time. If they are to be used for this purpose, they should be cut just before the buds open.

Pentstemon hybridus

Scrophulariaceae

GROENL. and RPL.

Beard Tongue

1 to 2 1/2 ft.

August to October

Pentstemon is a native of North America and Mexico. Many of the perennial species are of garden merit but the only one treated as an annual is *Pentstemon hybridus*. In the warm areas of Europe and America it will even live for several years. It is a sturdy, erect plant of bushy habit differing in height according to the variety. The leaves are sessile, pointed, coloured a deep glossy green. The large, bell-shaped flowers are arranged in attractive long spikes and are coloured white, pink, red, carmine or violet with a white throat sometimes spotted a different colour. The corolla of some flowers is edged with a wide border. The flowering season is from the end of July until late autumn, sometimes even to early November when all other flowers have been destroyed by frost. Pentstemon is offered in a mixture as well as in separate colours ('Scarlet Queen').

Pentstemon does best in moist, nourishing, sandy loam in a warm, sunny situation; it is intolerant of wet soil. The seeds should be sown in the greenhouse in boxes in February. Germination is slow, taking up to 3 weeks. Earlier flowering may be obtained by growing the plants in peat pots or the like. Seedlings may be moved out to their flowering positions as early as mid-April for they are not harmed by light frosts.

The long flowering period and attractive foliage make penstemon a good subject for the decoration of parks and public areas, where it is planted out in separate groups as well as singly in mixed beds. Cut flowers are striking in large vases but are suitable only for immediate use as they do not tolerate transport. The panicles should be cut when two-thirds of the flowers are in bloom. Flowers cut in the autumn last 6 to 8 days in water, but those cut in summer last only a short while.

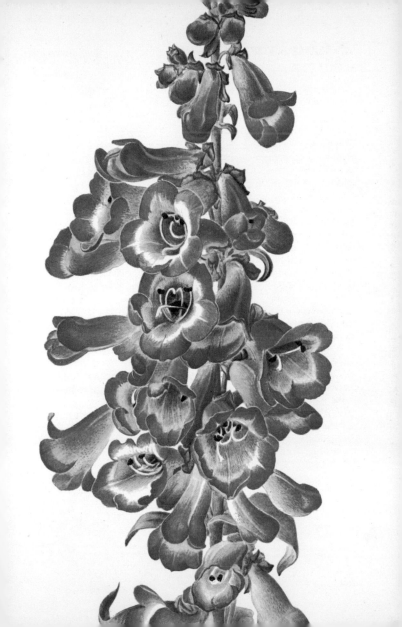

Petunia hybrida JUSS.

Solanaceae

8 to 32 in.

May to October

From the original species *Petunia nyctaginiflora* and *P. integrifolia,* both from Argentina, the modern hybrids *P. hybrida* have been raised. They are available in many different forms, both single and double, and in a wide range of colours excepting yellow. The varieties are divided into numerous groups and subgroups according to the height of the plant and type of flower. Best known are: *nana compacta* – 8 to 10 in., medium-large entire flowers; *grandiflora nana* – 8 to 10 in., flowers 2 1/2 to 3 1/2 in. across; *grandiflora fimbriata* – 12 to 14 in., large, ruffled flowers; *grandiflora fimbriata nana* – 10 to 14 in., frilled flowers of varying size; *superbissima* – 16 to 28 in., large, ruffled to frilled, bright-coloured flowers up to 4 1/2 in. across: 'Cascade' – trailing stems up to 32 in. long bearing a profusion of flowers 2 1/2 to 3 in. across. Some of the above groups also include double forms with like characteristics. In recent years certain groups are being replaced by F_1 hybrids, which are distinguished by uniformity of colour, floriferousness and resistance to unfavourable weather.

Petunias flourish in heavy, nourishing soil but will also grow in peat. They require a warm and airy situation.

The seeds should be sown in the greenhouse in boxes in February and the seedlings grown on in pots before planting outside. However, the home gardener will usually do better to buy plants from the nurseryman.

Petunias are among the most widely used annuals for window-box decoration and some of the newer hardy varieties can be used for the border.

Phacelia campanularia

Hydrophyllaceae

A. GRAY

California Bluebell

6 to 10 in.
June to July

Phacelia campanularia from North America is the only member of this genus of particular merit as an ornamental. It is an easily grown, early-flowering annual reaching a height of only 6 to 10 in. and of broadly branching, practically creeping habit. The rounded to heart-shaped leaves are irregularly notched and covered with a light down. The stem is reddish and the bell-shaped flowers, measuring about 1 in. across, are a brilliant gentian blue with 5 prominent white stamens. Phacelia blooms very early, within 7 to 8 weeks after sowing, from the beginning of June until the end of July if sown in April. The flowering period may be prolonged by sowing the seeds in succession. It is not only an attractive bedding plant but also a great attraction for bees.

Phacelia is very easy to cultivate and does well in any soil in a warm, sunny situation. The seeds should be sown directly into the open ground in pinches spaced 8 to 10 in. apart or else broadcast in early April. The seedlings should be thinned in time to a spacing of at least 6 in., leaving at most two plants together in one spot. The plants seed themselves readily and flowers are produced again in the autumn by the new seedlings.

Both the flowers and plants are comparatively small and thus are good for the mixed border, dry slopes beside paths, rock gardens and the like. The gentian blue colour – one that is not often found amongst annuals – always attracts merited attention. Because of its minimal requirements phacelia is useful for new, as yet unprepared ground where other plants would not thrive.

Phaseolus coccineus L.   *Viciaceae (Leguminosae)*
Syn. *Phaseolus multiflorus* LAM.

Bean

10 to 14 ft.
July to September

Phaseolus coccineus, a perennial treated as an annual, is the only bean grown as an ornamental. The firm stem, which always twines spirally upward from right to left and usually does not branch, grows to a height of 14 ft. The slightly hairy leaves are arranged 3 to a stalk and the small flowers, borne in loose clusters, are white, fiery red or else bicolored (the keel red, the wings white).

Phaseolus has no special requirements and will thrive in any garden soil. It does not tolerate frost and the seeds should therefore not be sown in the open until mid-April. The spacing should be about 12 in. Seeds may also be sown in pots and the seedlings planted out at the end of May. They should not be more than 12 in. tall. Plants sown directly into the open ground start bearing flowers at the beginning of July; those raised in pots and then planted out flower 3 weeks sooner. The plants should be provided with supports – either poles, wire, netting or twine. In periods of drought they must be watered for otherwise the leaves begin to turn yellow from the bottom up.

Phaseolus is a rapid-growing plant and therefore useful for quickly covering pergolas, fences, walls and the like. With the aid of a wooden or wire framework one can easily have a thick shaded screen in the patio, a divider for the garden or a cover for masking unsightly objects. Phaseolus is also used in balcony boxes.

Phlox drummondii HOOK.

Polemoniaceae

1/2 to 2 ft.

June to October

Phlox drummondii, from the southern United States, is the only species of this genus grown as an annual. It is a much-branched, free-flowering plant in practically all colours. When in full bloom the plant is entirely covered by the vast quantity of brilliant flowers. The many varieties are divided into several groups according to the size and form of the flower and height of the plant: *grandiflora* – 12 to 16 in. high; *nana compacta* – 6 to 8 in. high; *cuspidata* – dwarf form bearing small flowers with toothed margin. The flowering season is from the beginning of June throughout the summer.

Phlox requires a rich soil and warm, sunny position. It stands up well to dry conditions but is intolerant of damp soil and lengthy cold and rainy periods.

The seed should be sown in the greenhouse in boxes between mid-February and mid-March. Hardened-off seedlings may be moved to their outdoor positions as early as the middle of April for they are not harmed by light frosts. Seedlings planted out early branch better and also flower better than seedlings planted out at the end of May. Pinching out the growing points will promote bushier growth. The spacing between plants in their flowering positions should be 6 to 12 in., depending on the variety.

Phlox is good for the low border, rock garden and dry wall. Small groups of a single colour are very attractive in a mixed bed. Low-growing forms are used for planting in balcony boxes as well as in earthenware urns on the terrace. Taller forms may be used for cutting. They last 6 to 8 days in water; the buds open in succession.

Portulaca grandiflora HOOK.

Portulacaceae

Sun Plant, Rose Moss

4 to 6 in.

June to September

Portulaca grandiflora, a native of Argentina and Brazil, is a broadly spreading, dwarf plant of prostrate habit. In coloured forms the fleshy stem is reddish, in white forms green. The narrow, sessile leaves are also fleshy. The pretty flowers, single, semi-double and double, measure 1 1/2 in. across. The petals are wide with wavy margins and have a silky sheen. The colour range includes white, pale to deep yellow, pink to carmine, and orange to scarlet in many shades; flowers may also be striped in various colours. A single plant bears 10 to 12 open flowers at one time. Seedsmen's catalogues generally offer single- or double-flowered forms in mixtures. The flowers open only in full sun before noon, and are produced from June to August.

Portulaca does best in well-drained, sandy soil and in a warm, sunny position. It does not flower as well in the shade or in excessively rich soil and is intolerant of heavy, clay and wet soil. Long spells of rainy weather may completely destroy the plants.

The seeds should be sown in the greenhouse in boxes in February or March. They are very tiny and therefore should not be covered at all or only lightly with sand. Hardened-off seedlings may be moved outside, spaced 8 to 12 in. apart, in late May after all danger of frost is past. If conditions are favourable the seeds may be sown directly into open ground at the end of April. The outcome is sometimes rather uncertain but often very good plants will grow in the same site from self-sown seed.

Portulaca is used for the border, dry, sunny slopes, rock gardens as well as for the patio and balcony boxes. Often it is very useful for brightening places where, because of excessively dry conditions and insufficient soil, most other plants would have very poor growth.

Reseda odorata L.

Mignonette

Resedaceae

10 to 16 in.

July to September

Of great merit as an ornamental plant is the species *Reseda odorata*, which grows wild in North Africa. The plants make a bushy growth of broadly spreading to almost creeping habit. The small, delightfully fragrant flowers are arranged in thick, broad spikes and are coloured green or yellow-green with striking red or yellow anthers. The flowering period is from July until late autumn. The best known forms are 'Goliath' – 1 ft. high, flowers with deep-red anthers; 'Machet' – 16 in. high with dark foliage and pale red flowers.

Mignonette requires good nourishing soil and a warm, sunny situation, but will tolerate light shade. It responds well to the addition of well-rotted farmyard manure to the soil in the autumn. Excessively wet and heavy soil, however, is detrimental.

The seeds should be sown directly in the open ground, in rows 10 to 12 in. apart, in early spring.

The flowers are insignificant but have a penetrating scent and are grown mainly in country gardens for their delicious fragrance and as food for bees. Reseda is also planted sometimes for the restful effect of its deep green foliage amidst the bright colours of other annuals. It may also be grown in flowerpots.

204

Ricinus communis L.

Castor Oil Plant, Castor Bean

Euphorbiaceae

5 to 10 ft.

Ricinus communis embraces many forms differing in height, colouring of the leaves and shape of the seed. The original form, probably a native of Africa or East India, is nowadays grown in all warmer regions. In central Europe it can be grown only as an annual for it will not survive even the mildest winter. If conditions are favourable the huge plants may grow to a height of 10 ft. The large leaves are palmate and differ in colour according to the variety. The flowers are borne in thick panicles; it is the leaves, not the flowers, however, that are the plant's ornamental feature. Of the many formerly available varieties, only two or three are offered nowadays (listed under their botanical names), generally *sanguineus* – up to 7 ft. high with dark red fruits and leaves; *zanzibarensis* – 7 to 10 ft. high with glossy green leaves; and *gibsonii* – up to 5 ft. high with dark red foliage.

Ricinus requires sandy loam and a sunny situation. The seeds should be sown directly into small pots in mid-March. They may be sown even earlier but then the plants must be potted on before being moved to their permanent positions. The seeds will germinate more quickly and more readily if soaked in tepid water for one day prior to sowing. The seedlings should be planted outdoors after all danger of frost is past. Well-rotted compost should be added to the soil where the seedlings are put and fertiliser should be subsequently applied at regular intervals and the plants watered liberally according to need.

Ricinus is planted out as a solitary subject or in groups in grass or in front of buildings. It is good as a backdrop for flowers, being generally used to mask walls and fences, but it is also used in large containers and earthenware urns, where it is very attractive even though it is not as large as when grown in the open ground.

Rudbeckia bicolor NUTT.

Asteraceae
(Compositae)

Coneflower

20 to 40 in.
July to October

All the varieties are distinguished by a great profusion of flowers borne over a very long period. The plants are of varying height, erect and of irregularly branching habit. The long, ovate-lanceolate leaves are rough and pale green in colour. The sturdy stems are about 18 in. long and are topped by daisy-like flowers 3 to 4 in. across with protruding, cone-shaped to cylindrical centres. The ray petals are lightly fluted, tapering to a point, and coloured deep yellow or yellow with a reddish-brown centre. The central disc in the fully open flower has a metallic sheen. A single stalk bears up to 60 flowers from mid-July until late autumn. They are not harmed by light frosts. Best known varieties are 'Kelvedon Star' – rich yellow, zoned mahogany with brown centre; 'Gloriosa Daisy' – with very large flowers of varying colours; 'My Joy' – golden yellow; and the more recent 'Irish Eyes' – yellow with green centre.

Rudbeckia does best in sandy loam rich in humus and in a warm, sunny position. The seeds should be sown in a frame in mid-March and the seedlings planted out where they are to flower in mid-May.

Rudbeckia is most attractive in the late summer and autumn months when its glowing colours provide a gay and joyous display in the garden. It may be planted in small or large clumps in the mixed bed, as a stop-gap between perennials and in front of shrubs or dark evergreens. It is also very good for cutting, the flowers lasting up to 14 days in water. They should be cut when fully open for the buds tend to wilt.

Salpiglossis sinuata RUIZ and PAV *Solanaceae*
Syn. *Salpiglossis grandiflora* HORT.
S. Variabilis HORT.
Trumpet Flower

16 to 32 in.
June to August

Only *Salpiglossis sinuata* from Chile is grown as an ornamental. It is a sparsely branching plant of upright habit, varying in height according to the variety. The trumpet-shaped flowers are in various colours, the main shades being white, yellow or rose-violet. The throat is usually darker, either red or violet, with prominent dark veins. The flowering season is from late June until late August. Of the many formerly cultivated varieties the ones generally offered nowadays are *grandiflora* or *superbissima* mixtures.

Salpiglossis requires a well-drained, nourishing soil and sunny, sheltered position. It is sometimes destroyed by strong winds and long rainy periods and it will not grow well in wet and heavy or excessively dry sandy soil.

The seeds should be sown in a frame at the end of March and the seedlings, which have been transferred to peat pots, planted out in their permanent positions, 8 to 12 in. apart, at the end of May. The seeds may also be sown directly into the open ground. However, as they are very small and the young seedlings very tender this method should be used only in a well-prepared bed and sheltered site. Even mature plants are very sensitive to caked soil, so the ground must be kept well hoed.

The elegant, brightly coloured flowers make this a very good subject for mixed beds near paths or in a small garden. The colours tend to merge when viewed from a distance, so it is best to plant them where they can be easily seen. Cut flowers last 4 to 7 days in water but do not tolerate lengthy transport.

Salvia farinacea BENTH.

Lamiaceae
(Labiatae)

Sage

1 1/2 to 3 ft.

June to October

Salvia farinacea from Texas is a perennial treated as an annual. It is a plant of upright, richly branching habit growing to a height of 3 ft. The small blue-violet or white flowers are arranged in thick whorls in a 7-in.-long spike and are produced from early June until late autumn. The seeds should be sown in a frame or in the greenhouse in early March. The seedlings, which grow best of all in peat pots, are planted out, 16 in. apart, at the end of May.

Salvia farinacea is very attractive when planted in large masses in parks and public areas and in smaller groups in the mixed border in the garden. The cut flowers are attractive in mixed floral arrangements.

Salvia horminum is a native of southern Europe. The separate small flowers, coloured white, carmine or violet, are rather insignificant but attractive, as are the similarly coloured bracts surrounding them. The plants reach a height of 18 in. The seeds should be sown under glass in March or April, or else directly into open ground in late April. It is planted in parks in separate groups.

Also good for park decoration is *Salvia coccinea* from the warm regions of North America. White-felted and of broadly branching habit, this plant grows to a height of 2 ft. The small, scarlet flowers are borne in loose spikes. The seeds should be sown in March and the seedlings planted out at the end of May.

All three sages flourish in any garden soil in a sunny position.

Salvia splendens KER. GAWL.

Lamiaceae
(Labiatae)

Scarlet Sage

8 to 14 in.
May to October

This sage is a perennial native to Brazil. The original form is no longer cultivated, but breeders have produced many attractive, generally low-growing varieties of compact habit. These erect plants with stout, branching stems have bright green, longish heart-shaped leaves with serrated margins. The labiate flowers with like-coloured calyx are arranged in a spike and open in succession. Most varieties are a brilliant scarlet but also offered are white, rose, salmon, lavender and blue-violet forms. Best known are 'Fireball' – 14 in.; 'St. John's Fire' – 10 in.' Bonfire' – 18 in.; and 'Red Hussar' – 12 in.' all bearing a wealth of brilliant scarlet flowers until the frosts. They are generally planted out when already in bloom.

The plants do best in good nourishing soil and in a sunny situation. However, pastel-coloured forms do better in semi-shade.

The seeds should be sown in the greenhouse in boxes in February. When large enough the seedlings are usually put into pots. They are then moved to their outdoor places, spaced 10 to 12 in. apart, but not before the end of May or beginning of June as they are very sensitive to frost. Since plants grown in larger pots transplant readily they can be put out in place of flowers that have already faded.

Salvia is one of the most widely used annuals for parks and public places. It is also very good for the mixed border and balcony boxes.

Sanvitalia procumbens LAM.

Asteraceae
(Compositae)

Creeping Zinnia

4 to 8 in.

June to October

Only this species, *Sanvitalia procumbens* from Mexico, is grown for garden decoration. A low, creeping plant, it spreads out to a width of 20 in. The stems are greatly branched and felted, the leaves pale green, egg-shaped and pointed. The small bright yellow flowers, borne in profusion, are either single with a large, purple-black centre or double, spherical, with pointed ray petals and a practically indiscernible centre. The flowering period often begins in late May and the blooms are produced continuously throughout the summer until destroyed by frosts.

Sanvitalia is easy to cultivate. It does best in light, well-drained soil in a warm, sunny position. The seeds should be sown in a frame in late March, but may also be sown directly in the open ground at the end of April. However, the first method is more reliable. The seedlings should be planted in their permanent positions, 1 ft. apart, at the end of May when all danger of frost is past, for the young plants are very sensitive to frost.

Sanvitalia is a very good subject for the rock garden, dry wall, dry, sunny slopes and borders alongside paths. It also grows very well in earthenware urns. Planted separately or together with blue annuals such as ageratum, lobelia or verbena, it makes an effective display in the garden throughout the summer.

Scabiosa atropurpurea DESF.

Sweet Scabious, Pincushion Flower

Dipsacaceae

16 to 36 in.

July to October

Scabiosa atropurpurea is a native of southern Europe. It is a slender, graceful plant with sparse foliage. The leaves, of varying size, are lance-shaped and shallowly toothed. The double varieties in shades of white, yellow, violet, pink, red and purple to purplish black as well as bicolored forms have been bred from the original purple form. The slender, firm, smooth stems may be as much as 3 ft. long. Varieties are classed according to height as dwarf – 16 in., intermediate – 2 ft., and tall – 3 ft. The flowering period is from the end of July until late autumn. Varieties are offered according to colour, for example 'Cherry Red', 'Blue Moon', 'Coral Moon' and mixed shades.

The sweet scabious has no special requirements and thrives in any garden soil, though it does best in light, well-drained soil with sufficient lime. Tall varieties require a sheltered position for they are easily uprooted or laid flat by strong winds.

The seeds should be sown in a frame in late March. The seedlings may be moved to their outdoor places, about 8 to 12 in. apart, in early May. Hardened-off seedlings are not damaged by mild frosts. The seeds may also be sown directly into the open ground but then flowering is quite late.

Tall plants are used mostly for cutting. The best time to cut the blooms is when they are about half-open. They will last 5 to 10 days in water and are very good as solitary subjects and in combination with other flowers. Dwarf and intermediate varieties are usually planted in the mixed border, between newly planted perennials, and the like. The glowing colours make them very effective as decoration.

Schizanthus wisetonensis LOW.

Solanaceae

10 to 16 in.

June to July

Of the several species native to Chile, the most frequently grown today is the hybrid *Schizanthus wisetonensis* resulting from the crossing of *S. pinnatus* and *S. grahamii* and probably still other species. The plants are compact and regularly branched with pale green, bipinnately compound leaves. Their habit of growth and delicate, fresh green foliage makes them a very attractive subject even before they flower. The flowers are symmetrical, with irregularly notched or nearly rounded corollas coloured white, pale pink, red or purple with a patch of contrasting colour marked with dark veining. Various mixtures are offered differing in the form and size of the flower and of the plant. The flowering season is fairly short – from the end of June until late July.

Schizanthus does best in nourishing, sandy loam with sufficient lime and in a warm, sunny situation. It is intolerant of fresh farmyard manure and is damaged by cold rainy weather.

The seeds should be sown in a frame in mid-March and the seedlings pricked out in time and far enough apart, for if left too close together they tend to grow tall and decay. Seedlings are best grown in pots and put out about 1 ft. apart at the end of May when all danger of frost is past.

Schizanthus is used for low, mixed beds, dry walls and rockeries as well as in earthenware urns. Cut flowers are highly decorative and last 7 to 10 days in water.

Silene pendula L.

Silenaceae
(Caryophyllaceae)

Catchfly

4 to 10 in.

July to August

Silene pendula from the Mediterranean is a plant of compact, broadly branching to prostrate habit, measuring up to 20 in. across, covered with a light down. The stems are reddish, the leaves longish ovate, rough and coloured bright green. The small flowers have a persistent calyx and deeply notched petals. They are either single or double and arranged in clusters, borne in such profusion that when in full bloom they entirely conceal the leaves. The colours are white, pink, glowing red or lavender blue. The flowering season is from the beginning of July until the end of August. Varieties are offered in separate colours, or in mixed colours, mostly double forms. Single forms, which are more than 20 in. across, are fairly sparse and cultivated only occasionally.

Silene has no special requirements and flourishes in any garden soil and in a warm, sunny situation. Lengthy periods of rain and waterlogged soil cause the plants to decay.

The seeds should be sown in a frame in March and the seedlings may be planted out, about 12 to 16 in. apart, at the end of April. Flowering may be delayed by the time of sowing. Silene seeds itself and often the plants flower early in spring.

It is used for fow borders, on dry slopes beside paths, as a solitary subject in the rock garden, in dry walls and also in earthenware urns on terraces.

Tagetes erecta L.

African Marigold

Asteraceae
(Compositae)

8 to 48 in.

July to October

Tagetes erecta from Mexico is a very widespread species from which new hybrids are being derived every year – tall, intermediate as well as dwarf. They are broadly branching plants with fresh green, feathered foliage that has a strong unpleasant scent, a drawback that has been overcome in new varieties. African marigolds are classed according to the form of the flower either as 'carnation flowered' – with tongue-shaped, frilled petals, or 'chrysanthemum-flowered' – with tube-shaped petals. They are only in shades of yellow and orange. Examples of tall varieties are 'Golden Glory' – yellow; 'Orange Prince' – orange, and 'Lemon Queen' – yellow; dwarfs include 'Cupid' and 'Spun Gold'. Offered in increasing numbers in recent years are modern F_1 hybrids that bear a great abundance of large flowers in glowing shades. Especially magnificent are the 'Climax' and 'Jubilee' strains.

African marigolds will grow in any garden soil but do best in soil with good drainage and in a warm, sunny position. They are intolerant of shade and flower poorly in excessively rich soil.

The seeds should be sown in a frame in rows in early April and the seedlings thinned after germination. They transplant very well. Seeds should not be sown too early. The seedlings must not be too close together and ample ventilation is important. Plants should be moved to their flowering positions at the end of May. The spacing for dwarf varieties should be 8 in., for tall varieties 12 to 16 in.

Dwarf and intermediate varieties are good as solitary subjects or in groups in the border and also in flower pots and earthenware urns. Tall varieties are used mostly for cutting, the flowers lasting 8 to 15 days in water.

224

Tagetes patula L.

French Marigold

Asteraceae
(Compositae)

8 to 18 in.

June to October

Tagetes patula from Mexico makes a low, densely branched semi-globular bush of compact habit. The flowers are small, only 1 to 2 in. across, but are produced in great abundance (double forms bear up to 100 and single forms up to 200 flowers) and completely conceal the leaves when in full bloom. As the flowers fade new ones continually open so that the plants are decorative throughout the summer. They also stand up well to poor weather. French marigolds are divided into groups according to height, form of the flower, and type of flower. The flowering season is from June until autumn. The colour range is the same as for *T. erecta* but in addition includes shades of brownish-red and bicolored forms. Examples of double varieties are 'Fireflame' and 'Petite'; single varieties 'Lemon King', 'Dainty Marietta', 'Fire Cross' and 'Flash'.

Tagetes tenuifolia (syn. *T. signata*) has only a few varieties. It makes a branching plant with thick, pleasantly orange-scented foliage coloured a bright green. During the flowering period the dense, compact, semi-globular bush is entirely covered with small blossoms measuring 3/4 in. across and produced continually from July until the first frosts. The yellow and orange varieties have long been widely grown and to these has now been added a brown-red variety.

The soil requirements, situation and method of cultivation for both these species are the same as for *Tagetes erecta*.

The dwarf marigolds are among the most widely used annuals for parks and the decoration of public areas, where they are planted in separate groups or as edging plants. Seedlings grown in pots can be used for planting out after other flowers have faded.

Tithonia rotundifolia

(MILL.) BLAKE

Syn. *Tithonia speciosa* (ROOK) GRISEB.

Mexican Sunflower

Asteraceae

(Compositae)

4 to 6 ft.

August to October

Tithonia rotundifolia from Mexico is a vigorous, erect, branching plant with thick foliage growing to a height of 6 ft. if conditions are favourable. The long-stalked leaves are a deep, dark green, longish heart-shaped and slightly hairy. The numerous large, single flowers, up to 2 in. across, have long stems and are borne in succession. The relatively large ray petals are a rich orange-red, yellow on the underside, and the central disc is yellow. The flowers resemble a single dahlia but are more brightly coloured and have a delicate fragrance. They are borne from August until the first frosts.

Tithonia requires a nourishing, sandy loam and a warm, sheltered position, for it may be greatly damaged by strong winds.

The seeds should be sown in a frame in late March. The seedlings should be pricked out thinly or else may be grown in peat pots. They should be moved to their flowering positions, 20 to 24 in. apart, fairly late – at the end of May or beginning of June – for they are very sensitive to frost.

Tithonia is planted out either in separate groups or as a solitary subject in grass and to mask walls and fences. It may also be used as a temporary, rapid-growing green cover for large unsightly areas. The cut flowers are very attractive and long-lived, lasting 7 to 10 days in water. However, they do not tolerate transport as the stems, though quite sturdy, break easily just below the flower.

228

Tropaeolum majus L.

Nasturtium

Tropaeolaceae

10 in. to 10 ft.

June to October

This pretty annual, native to the mountain regions of South America, has given rise to many garden forms, all listed under *Tropaeolum majus*, even though most are hybrids of several species. The fleshy, branching plants are thickly covered with rounded, shield-like leaves on long stalks. The foliage is generally pale green, though some varieties have brownish-red foliage. The large, symmetrical flowers on long, slender stems are coloured yellow, salmon pink, scarlet or brownish-red, and may be single or double. Varieties are classed according to growth as either climbers – with up to 10-ft.-long stems, or dwarfs – semi-globular, bushy plants 10 to 12 in. high with thick foliage. The flowering season is from mid-June until late autumn, when the blooms are generally destroyed by the first frost. Best known varieties are 'Scarlet Gleam', 'Orange Gleam', 'Salmon Baby' and 'Cherry Rose'.

Nasturtium thrives in any garden soil and in a warm, sunny position. It flowers very well in poor stony soil; excessively rich soil promotes lush leaf growth which hides the flowers.

The seeds should be sown directly into the open ground, best of all in pinches, 12 to 20 in. apart, at the beginning of May. Earlier flowering may be attained by growing the seedlings in peat pots in a frame. Because they are sensitive to frost, they should not be planted out until the end of May.

Dwarf varieties are planted separately in the border, in mixed beds and in grass. They are also good for earthenware urns and balcony boxes. Climbing varieties are used for balconies as well as beside fences and railings. They also provide a rapid green cover for unsightly areas. The buds open well in water and last up to 10 days, thus serving as an attractive and inexpensive home decoration.

Ursinia anethoides (DC) N. E. BR.   *Asteraceae (Compositae)*

12 to 20 in.

July to August

Ursinia anethoides from South Africa is a branching plant of compact habit with graceful, feathery foliage coloured pale green. The single, daisy-like flowers on long, firm stems measure 2 in. across and are a brilliant orange with a central disc of the same colour encircled by a brownish-violet zone. The flowers are produced in great profusion (as many as 60 to a plant) from the beginning of July until the middle of August.

Ursinia does best in sandy, well-drained soil and in a warm, sunny situation. It is intolerant of wet soil; long periods of rain completely destroy the plants.

The seeds should be sown in a frame in early April and the seedlings may be planted out in their flowering positions, 8 to 12 in. apart, in mid-May. If conditions are favourable the seeds may be sown directly into the open ground at the end of April.

Ursinia is planted in separate borders as well as in mixed beds. It is suitable for the rock garden, dry wall and dry slopes. It is an attractive ornamental not only prior to and during the flowering period but even after the flowers have faded, when the white, star-like membranous wings of the seed cases make it seem as if it had flowered anew.

Venidium fastuosum STAPF.

Namaqualand Daisy, Monarch of the Veldt

Asteraceae
(Compositae)

2 to 3 ft.

June to October

The original species, an interesting annual from South Africa, is no longer cultivated, having been superseded by its hybrids *Venidium fastuosum* hort. The plants are of broadly spreading habit with erect, branching stems thickly covered with downy hairs and measuring up to 20 in. The longish, lyre-shaped leaves are also hairy, grey-green, and sparse. The large flowers, measuring 3 to 4 in. across, have white or orange ray petals and shiny, dark brown to black centres, encircled by a deep violet and orange zone. When open the blooms are very attractive but in rainy weather or dull light they close. As many as 50 flowers are borne in succession on a single plant from mid-June until late autumn, the first mild frosts usually causing no damage.

Venidium requires nourishing, well-drained soil and a warm, sunny position. In wet soil and locations with frequent rainfall the plants decay.

The seeds should be sown in a frame at the beginning of April. Growth is very rapid and if sown too early or too thickly the seedlings grow too tall. They may be planted out in their permanent positions, about 16 in. apart, in early May. Hardened-off seedlings are not damaged by light spring frosts.

Venidium is suitable for the country garden or in small groups for the mixed bed. One should keep in mind that the plants are of fairly broad, spreading habit.

Verbena hybrida VOSS.

Vervain

Verbenaceae

8 to 18 in.

June to October

Both the annual and perennial species of the genus *Verbena,* native to North and South America, produce continuous flowers. Multiple crossing of the species has given rise to *Verbena hybrida.* The plants are much branched, erect and of spreading as well as trailing habit, making either globular and compact or flat and broad bushy growths. The branching lateral stems are terminated by thick round heads of flowers measuring 2 to 2 1/2 in. across and containing 16 to 20 small, pleasantly scented flowers. They are in all shades except yellow, either a single colour or with a white eye. Taller varieties belong to the 'Mammoth' group (14 to 18 in), dwarf varieties to the 'Compacta' group (8 to 10 in.). They flower from June until the frosts.

Verbena has no special requirements and thrives in any good garden soil and in a warm, sunny, sheltered situation. It grows and flowers well even in poor soil if fertiliser is supplied during the growth period. Cold and rainy weather is detrimental.

The seeds should be sown in the greenhouse in boxes at the beginning of March. The seedlings usually need to be pricked out twice and after hardening off may be planted out at the end of May. They are sensitive to frost.

Verbena is a very good ornamental for parks and public areas. It is also very attractive in the small garden and useful as a bedding plant, for edging purposes and in window boxes.

Verbena bonariensis

Verbenaceae

12 to 40 in.

June to October

Other verbenas cultivated in addition to *Verbena hybrida* include those listed below, also originating from America.

Verbena bonariensis is an upright, branching, bushy plant up to 40 in. high. The erect, 4-sided, rigid stems are practically leafless so that the plants create a light, airy effect despite their size. The heads of small flowers are lilac blue and are borne from July until the frosts. This verbena is planted together with tall annuals or perennials in the border as well as in separate groups in grass or between shrubs. The cut blooms are also attractive for floral arrangements.

Verbena canadensis (syn. *V. aubletia*) is 8 to 12 in. high and makes a compact, globular plant up to 12 in. across. The asymmetrically lobed leaves are notched and pale green in colour. The dense, rosy-lilac flower heads measure up to 2 in. across and are borne from the beginning of June until the autumn. The uses of this species are the same as for *V. hybrida*.

Invaluable for park decoration is *Verbena rigida* (syn. *V. venosa*), a 12- to 16-in.-high plant of loose, broadly spreading habit with dense foliage. The pointed, toothed leaves have a rough upper surface and the pale violet flowers, arranged in a spike, open in succession.

Verbena erinoides is a 12- to 20-in.-high plant of greatly branching habit with finely cut leaves and small, blue-violet flowers resembling those of *V. rigida*. It may be grown on poor soil.

All four species have the same requirements as regards soil and location as *V. hybrida*. *V. rigida*, however, takes a longer time to germinate (from 3 to 4 weeks).

238

Viola wittrockiana GAMS.

Syn. *Viola tricolor* HORT.
V. t. maxima HORT.

Pansy, Viola

Violaceae

4 to 10 in.
April to July

Of the many species of *Viola* growing wild in nearly all parts of the world, the one cultivated in our gardens is the multiple hybrid *Viola wittrockiana*. The currently grown varieties are branching plants that make a compact bush. Sometimes, however, they are of prostrate to trailing habit. The flowers are symmetrical and differ in size (2 to 3 in.) according to the given variety. They are in all colours excepting bright red. Small-flowered forms produce a greater number of blooms than the large-flowered varieties. An important characteristic of these plants is their hardiness. Varieties are divided into groups according to the period of flowering. Early-flowering forms bloom in the autumn and in early spring and cease flowering in May. Later and late-flowering varieties produce blooms from April until August.

Violas need nourishing, humus-rich soil and a sheltered, sunny position. The seeds should be sown in the frame in mid-July and should be kept uniformly moist and shaded until they germinate. If sown thinly seedlings need not be pricked out. In late August or early September they may be moved outdoors to their permanent positions about 10 in. apart. Generally, however, they are first put in a nursery bed, 6 to 8 in. apart, and then transplanted in late autumn or early spring.

Violas are planted in large masses in parks and public areas either separately as a decorative element or together with other flowers. They are also used for earthenware urns and balcony boxes.

Xanthisma texanum DC.

Asteraceae
(Compositae)

Star of Texas

1 1/2 to 3 ft.

July to October

The only species of merit as an ornamental is *Xanthisma texanum* from Texas. It is of broadly spreading habit and the lateral stems are thickly covered with narrow, lance-shaped leaves. The daisy-like flowers, measuring 2 to 2 1/2 in. across, are a bright yellow with a pale yellow centre. They are borne in great profusion, as many as 90 to a single plant. New blooms are continually growing in to take the place of those that haved faded so that the effect is fresh and attractive over a long period.

Xanthisma has no special requirements but does best in sandy, well-drained soil and in a warm, sunny position. It is intolerant of waterlogged soil and is also damaged by cold and damp during the growth period.

The seeds should be sown in a frame or in boxes in mid-March and the seedlings moved out to their permanent positions about 14 to 16 in. apart in mid-May. Mature plants are fairly hardy.

Both the flowers and thick foliage make this a very decorative plant. However, despite the fact that it flowers throughout the summer (few annuals have such a long flowering period) xanthisma still remains a rarely grown plant. It is used for mixed beds and dry slopes. The cut flowers last 7 to 9 days in water.

Xeranthemum annuum L.

Asteraceae
(Compositae)

20 to 26 in.

July to October

Xeranthemum annuum, which grows wild in southern England, is a bushy plant with narrow, pointed leaves covered with a greyish down. The flowers are fairly small (1 1/2 in across), single or double, flat or globular, composed of numerous tubular florets and several rows of incurved bracts resembling petals. Both are the same colour, which may be white, rose, violet or purple. A single plant may produce as many as 130 of these flowers, borne continuously from the beginning of July until late autumn. The plants are not harmed by the first frosts.

Xeranthemum is of easy cultivation and flourishes in any good, well-drained soil and dry situation. It is intolerant of wetness.

The seeds should be sown in a frame in early March. Hardened-off seedlings may be moved into the open at the beginning of May as they are not damaged by frost. They should be spaced 12 to 16 in. apart and, if necessary, provided with protection against hares and rabbits.

Xeranthemum is used on dry slopes exposed to direct sunlight. When dried, the flowers are very good for winter decoration together with other everlastings. They should be cut as soon as they open and hung in small bunches upside-down to dry in a dark and well-ventilated room.

Zinnia elegans JACQ.

Asteraceae
(Compositae)

1 to 3 ft.

June to October

Zinnia elegans is a native of Mexico and parent of a great number of modern varieties which are divided into several groups according to height and form of flower. The plants are rough, branching, and of varying height. The erect, forked stems break off fairly easily. The flowers show marked diversity in size (2 to 6 in.), form and fullness of the blooms as well as in colour, the range including practically all shades excepting blue. The best-known groups are Dahlia-flowered, 'California Giants' and 'Lilliput'. In recent years the selection has been augmented by a great many more groups.

Less widely grown are the various varieties of *Zinnia angustifolia* (syn. *Z. haageana*), which are smaller (12 to 20 in.) and of looser, sparser habit but very floriferous. The single as well as double blooms measure 1 1/2 to 2 1/4 in. across and are generally multicoloured. Best known forms are 'Persian Carpet' and 'Old Mexico'. The earliest varieties begin flowering in late June and produce flowers until the frosts.

Zinnia does best in nourishing, humus-rich soil with good drainage and in a sunny, sheltered situation. Tall forms grown in an open site are often greatly damaged by strong winds when in full bloom.

The seeds should be sown in a frame in rows at the end of March. If thinly sown, the seedlings need not be pricked out. Those that have grown too tall may have their growing point removed. They should be moved to their outdoor positions, 10 to 16 in. apart, at the end of May.

Dwarf and intermediate varieties are good for the small garden as well as in larger masses in parks. Tall varieties are grown mostly for cutting; cut flowers last 6 to 10 days in water.

INDEX OF COMMON NAMES

INDEX OF LATIN NAMES